Ground Work

by the same author

The New York Trilogy
In the Country of Last Things
The Invention of Solitude
Moon Palace

Ground Work
Selected Poems and Essays 1970–1979

Paul Auster

faber and faber
LONDON · BOSTON

First published in 1990
by Faber and Faber Limited
3 Queen Square London WC1N 3AU

Photoset by Wilmaset Birkenhead Wirral
Printed in Great Britain by
Richard Clay Ltd Bungay Suffolk

All rights reserved

© Paul Auster, 1990

The selection of poems in this book reproduces
the contents of *Disappearances: Selected Poems
1970–1979* (Overlook, 1988), which was in turn
culled from the following books, previously
published in the USA:
Unearth (Living Hand, 1974)
Wall Writing (The Figures, 1976)
Fragments from Cold (Parenthèse, 1977)
White Spaces (Station Hill, 1980)
Facing the Music (Station Hill, 1980)
'Spokes' originally appeared in *Poetry*.

Most of the essays in this book were first
published in *The Art of Hunger* (The Menard
Press, London, 1982). They originally appeared
in the following magazines in the USA: *The New
York Review of Books, Parnassus, Commentary,
Montemora, Parenthèse, Studies in Twentieth
Century Literature, American Letters and
Commentary*.

A CIP record for this book is
available from the British Library

ISBN 0–571–14153–6

Contents

Poems

I: *1970–1972*
Spokes   3
Unearth   7

II: *1972–1975*
White Nights   29
Matrix and Dream   30
Interior   31
Pulse   32
Scribe   33
Choral   34
Meridian   35
Lackawanna   36
Lies. Decrees. 1972.   37
Ecliptic. Les Halles.   38
Dictum: After Great Distances   39
Fore-shadows   40
Ireland   41
Prism   42
Wall Writing   43
Covenant   44
Hieroglyph   46
White   47
Pastoral   48
Incendiary   49
Song of Degrees   50
Fire Speech   52
Lapsarian   53
Late Summer   55
Heraclitian   56

Braille 57
Salvage 58
Autobiography of the Eye 59
All Souls 60

III: *1975–1977*
Disappearances 61
Northern Lights 69
Reminiscence of Home 70
Effigies 71
Gnomon 73
Fragment from Cold 74
Aubade 75
Transfusion 77
Siberian 78
Clandestine 79
Quarry 80

IV: *1978–1979*
White Spaces 81
Credo 89
Obituary in the Present Tense 90
Narrative 91
S. A. 1911–1979 92
Search for a Definition 93
Between the Lines 96
In Memory of Myself 97
Bedrock 98
Facing the Music 99

Essays

The Art of Hunger 105
Pages for Kafka 116
New York Babel 119
Black on White 127
Dada Bones 129
Truth, Beauty, Silence 136

From Cakes to Stones   147
The Poetry of Exile   153
The Death of Sir Walter Ralegh   164
Innocence and Memory   170
Northern Lights   178
Book of the Dead   183
The Decisive Moment   211

Poems

I: 1970–1972

Spokes

Roots writhe with the worm – the sift
Of the clock cohabits the sparrow's heart.
Between branch and spire – the word
Belittles its nest, and the seed, rocked
By simpler confines, will not confess.
Only the egg gravitates.

*

In water – my absence in aridity. A flower.
A flower that defines the air.
In the deepest well, your body is fuse.

*

The bark is not enough. It furls
Redundant shards, will barter
Rock for sap, blood for veering sluice,
While the leaf is pecked, brindled
With air, and how much more, furrowed
Or wrapped, between dog and wolf,
How much longer will it stake
The axe to its gloating advantage?

*

Nothing waters the bole, the stone wastes nothing.
Speech could not cobble the swamp,
And so you dance for a brighter silence.
Light severs wave, sinks, camouflages –
The wind clacks, is bolt.
I name you desert.

*

Picks jot the quarry – eroded marks
That could not cipher the message.
The quarrel unleashed its alphabet,
And the stones, girded by abuse,
Have memorized the defeat.

*

Drunk, whiteness hoards its strength,
When you sleep, sun drunk, like a seed
That holds its breath
Beneath the soil. To dream in heat
All heat
That infests the equilibrium
Of a hand, that germinates
The miracle of dryness . . .
In each place you have left
Wolves are maddened
By the leaves that will not speak.
To die. To welcome red wolves
Scratching at the gates: howling
Page – or you sleep, and the sun
Will never be finished.
It is green where black seeds breathe.

*

The flower is red, is perched
Where roots split, in the gnarl
Of a tower, sucking in its meager fast,
And retracting the spell
That welds step to word
And ties the tongue to its faults.
The flower will be red
When the first word tears the page,
Will thrive in the ooze, take color,
Of a lesioned beak, when the sparrow
Is bloodied, and flies from one
Earth into the bell.

*

Between the sparrow and the bird without name:
its prey.

Light escapes through the interval.

>   *

Each trance pales in the hub, the furtive
Equinox of names: pawl
Thwarting ratchet – jarring skies that orb
This austere commerce with wind.
Lulls mend. But gales nourish
Chance: breath, blooming, while the wheel scores
Its writing into earth. Bound back
To your feet. Eyes tend soil
In the cool of dying suns. The song
Is in the step.

>   *

Embering to the lip
Of nether sky – the undevoured nest-light
Ebbs to sustenance: from the sparrow
To the bird without name, the interval
Is prey – smoke
That softens coals, unlike the sect
Of wings, where you beat, smoke wed
To glow – in the sparrow's memory
It perfects the sleep of clouds.

>   *

To see is this other torture, atoned for
In the pain of being seen: the spoken,
The seen, contained in the refusal
To speak, and the seed of a single voice,
Buried in a random stone.
My lies have never belonged to me.

>   *

Into the hub the shell implodes,
Endures as a pun of loam and rock,
Rising as stick, to invade, to drive
Out the babble that worded its body
To emerge, to wait for future
Blows – city in root, in deed, unsprung, even out
Of the city. Get out. The wheel
Was deception. It cannot turn.

*

The egg limits renunciation, cannot
Sound in another's ringing, the least
Hammering, before the wail slits
Its course, and the eye squanders
The subterfuge of a longer lamp.
Lifted into speech, it carries
Its own birth, and if it shatters
Acclaim its fall and contradiction.
Your earth will always be far.

Unearth

1 Along with your ashes, the barely
written ones, obliterating
the ode, the incited roots, the alien
eye – with imbecilic hands, they dragged you
into the city, bound you in
this knot of slang, and gave you
nothing. Your ink has learned
the violence of the wall. Banished,
but always to the heart
of brothering quiet, you cant the stones
of unseen earth, and smooth your place
among the wolves. Each syllable
is the work of sabotage.

11 Flails, the whiteness, the flowers
of the promised land: and all
you hoard, crumbling at the brink
of breath. For a single word
in air we have not breathed, for one
stone, splitting with the famine
inside us – ire,
out of bone's havoc, by which we kin
the worm. The wall
is your only witness. Barred
from me, but squandering nothing,
you sprawl over each unwritten page,
as though your voice had crawled
from you: and entered the whiteness
of the wail.

III Vatic lips, weaned
of image. The mute one
here, who waits, urn-wise,
in wonder. Curse overbrims
prediction: the glacial rose
bequeaths its thorns to the breath
that labors toward eye
and oblivion.
We have only to ready ourselves.
From the first step, our voice
is in league
with the stones of the field.

IV Night, as though tasted
within. And of us, each lie
the tongue would know
when it draws back, and sinks
into its poison.
We would sleep, side by side
with such hunger, and from the fruit
we war with, become the name
of what we name. As though a crime, dreamed
by us, could ripen in cold, and fell
these black, roweling trees
that drain the history of stars.

v Unquelled
in this flood of earth –
where seeds end
and augur nearness – you will sound
the choral rant
of memory, and go the way
that eyes go. There is no longer
path for you: from the moment
you slit your veins, roots will begin
to recite the massacre
of stones. You will live. You will build
your house here – you will forget
your name. Earth
is the only exile.

VI Thistle, drenched by heat,
and the barren word
that prods you – shouted
down to the lodes.
Light would spill here.
It would seep through
the scrawled branch that wrote
such cowering above us.
As if, far from you,
I could feel it breaking
through me, as I walked
north into my body.

VII Between these spasms
of light, in brittle fern, in dark
thickets: waiting
in your labyrinthine ear
for the thunder
to crack: for the Babel-roar,
for the silence. It will not
be what you wandered to
that is heard. But the step,
burrowing under
this parted sky, that keeps its distance
whole. And that widens in you
at the mouth
of cloven earth, where you watch
these fallen stars
struggle to crawl back to you,
bearing the gifts of hell.

VIII Ice – means nothing
is miracle, if it must
be what will – you are the means
and the wound – opening
out of ice, and the cadence through
blunt earth, when crows
come to maraud. Wherever you walk, green
speaks into you, and holds. Silence
stands the winter eye to eye
with spring.

IX Scrolls of your second earth, unraveled
by my slow, incendiary hands.
The sky in your name – sliding down
scarps of blueness: the sky
overroaring wheat.
Do not ask – for what. Say nothing –
watch. Parades of the beaten,
for whom I tore apart
the drum. Your other life, glowing in the fuse
of this one. The unbaked loaves: the retina's lack
of solace.

x Wind-spewn, from the radiant
no, and grafted on
the brown-green scar of this
moment. You ask
what place this is, and I, along the seams
of your dismembering,
have told you: the forest
is the memory
of itself, this frail
splinter, streaming through
my navigable blood, and driven
aground in heart-rubble. You ask
words of me, and I
will speak them – from the moment
I have learned
to give you nothing.

XI From one stone touched
to the next stone
named: earth-hood: the inaccessible
ember. You
will sleep here, a voice
moored to stone, moving through
this empty house that listens
to the fire that destroyed it. You
will begin. To drag your body
from the ashes. To carry the burden
of eyes.

XII Prayer-grown –
in the ghost-written tract
of your somewhere,
in the landscape
where you will not stand – whorl-bits
of ammonite
reinvent you.
They roll you along
with earth's mock caroling
underfoot, scattering
the hundred-faced lie
that makes you visible. And from each
daylight blow, your hardness turns
to weapon, another slum
flowers within. (Prayer-grown –
the clandestine word, as though cutting
through the hand
that groped along these cave walls): wherever
I do not find you, the silent
mob that drifted mouthward – throngs
loudly into time.

XIII River-noises, cool. A remnant
grief, merging
with the not yet nameable.
Barge wake, silt, and autumn. Head-
waters churn, a strand
of kelp
wheels over the rank
whey of foam – as one, nail-pierced
shard, twice, floats past you, salvaging
asylum
in eyes washed clean
of bliss.

xiv Mirrored by the tent-speech
of our forty-dark, alodial-hued
next year –
the images,
ground in the afterlight
of eyes, the wandered
images absolve you: (dunes
that whirled free, – scree-words
shuttled
by the grate of sand, – the other
glass-round hours, redoubling
in remembrance). And in
my hand – (as, after the night, – the night) –
I hold what you have taken
to give: this path
of tallied cries, and grain
after grain, the never-done-with
desert, burning on your lips
that jell in violence.

xv Frail dawn: the boundary
of your darkened lamp: air
without word: a rose-round, folding
corolla of ash. From the smallest
of your suns, you clench
the scald: husk
of relented light: the true seed
in your fallow palm, deepening
into dumbness. Beyond this hour, the eye
will teach you. The eye will learn
to long.

XVI Notched out
on this crust of field – in the day
that comes after us,
where you saw the earth
almost happen again: the echoing
furrows have closed,
and for this one-more-life, have ransomed you
against the avid murmur
of scythes. Count me along, then,
with your words. Nothing,
even on this day, will change.
Shoulder
to shoulder with dust, before
the blade, and beyond
the tall dry grass
that veers with me, I am the air's
stammered relic.

XVII Evening, at half-mast
through mulberry-glow and lichen: the banner
of the unpronounceable
future. The skull's
rabble
crept out from you – doubling
across the threshold – and became
your knell
among the many: you
never heard it
again. Anti-stars
above the city you expel
from language, turning, at odds,
even with you, repeal the arson-
eye's quiet
testimony.

XVIII Rats wake in your sleep
and mime the progress
of want. My voice turns back
to the hunger it gives birth to,
coupling with stones
that jut from red walls: the heart
gnaws, but cannot know
its plunder; the flayed tongue
rasps. We lie
in earth's deepest marrow, and listen
to the breath of angels.
Our bones have been drained.
Wherever night has spoken,
unborn sons prowl the void
between stars.

XIX The dead still die: and in them
the living. All space,
and the eyes, hunted
by brittle tools, confined
to their habits.
To breathe is to accept
this lack of air, the only breath,
sought in the fissures
of memory, in the lapse that sunders
this language of feuds, without which earth
would have granted a stronger omen
to level the orchards
of stone. Not even
the silence pursues me.

xx Immune to the craving
gray of fog, hate, uttered
in the eaves, day-
long, kept you near. We
knew that sun
had wormed through the shuttered panes
in drunkenness
only. We knew a deeper void
was being
built by the gulls who scavenged
their own cries. We knew that they
knew the landfall
was mirage.
And was waiting,
from the first hour
I had come to you. My skin,
shuddering in the light.
The light, shattering at my touch.

XXI No one's voice, alien
to fall, and once
gathered in the eye that bled
such brightness. Your sinew
does not mend, it is
another rope, braided
by ink, and aching through
this raw hand – that hauls the images
back to us: the clairvoyant
corpse, singing
from his gallows-mirror; a glance,
heavier than stone, hurled
down to April
ice, ringing the bottom
of your breath-well; an eye,
and then
one more. Till vulture
is the word
that gluts this offal, night
will be your prey.

XXII Nomad –
till nowhere, blooming
in the prison of your mouth, becomes
wherever you are: you
read the fable
that was written in the eyes
of dice: (it was
the meteor-word, scrawled by light
between us, yet we, in the end,
had no evidence, we
could not produce
the stone). The die-and-the-die
now own your name. As if to say,
wherever you are
the desert is with you. As if,
wherever you move, the desert
is new,
is moving with you.

II: 1972–1975

White Nights

No one here,
and the body says: whatever is said
is not to be said. But no one
is a body as well, and what the body says
is heard by no one
but you.

Snowfall and night. The repetition
of a murder
among the trees. The pen
moves across the earth: it no longer knows
what will happen, and the hand that holds it
has disappeared.

Nevertheless, it writes.
It writes: in the beginning,
among the trees, a body came walking
from the night. It writes:
the body's whiteness
is the color of earth. It is earth,
and the earth writes: everything
is the color of silence.

I am no longer here. I have never said
what you say
I have said. And yet, the body is a place
where nothing dies. And each night,
from the silence of the trees, you know
that my voice
comes walking toward you.

Matrix and Dream

Inaudible things, chipped
nightly away:
breath, underground
through winter: well-words
down the quarried light
of lullaby rill
and chasm.

You pass.
Between fear and memory,
the agate
of your footfall turns
crimson
in the dust of childhood.

Thirst: and coma: and leaf –
from the gaps
of the no longer known: the unsigned message,
buried in my body.

The white linen
hanging on the line. The wormwood
crushed
in the field.

The smell of mint
from the ruin.

Interior

Grappled flesh
of the fully other and one.
And each thing here, as if it were the last thing
to be said: the sound of a word
married to death, and the life
that is this force in me
to disappear.

Shutters closed. The dust
of a former self, emptying the space
I do not fill. This light
that grows in the corner of the room,
where the whole of the room
has moved.

Night repeats. A voice that speaks to me
only of smallest things.
Not even things – but their names.
And where no names are –
of stones. The clatter of goats
climbing through the villages
of noon. A scarab
devoured in the sphere
of its own dung. And the violet swarm
of butterflies beyond.

In the impossibility of words,
in the unspoken word
that asphyxiates,
I find myself.

Pulse

This that recedes
will come near to us
on the other side of day.

Autumn: a single leaf
eaten by light: and the green
gaze of green upon us.
Where earth does not stop,
we, too, will become this light,
even as the light
dies
in the shape of a leaf.

Gaping eye
in the hunger of day.
Where we have not been
we will be. A tree
will take root in us
and rise in the light
of our mouths.

The day will stand before us.
The day will follow us
into the day.

Scribe

The name
never left his lips: he talked himself
into another body: he found his room again
in Babel.

It was written.
A flower
falls from his eye
and blooms in a stranger's mouth.
A swallow
rhymes with hunger
and cannot leave its egg.

He invents
the orphan in tatters,

he will hold
a small black flag
riddled with winter.

It is spring,
and below his window
he hears
a hundred white stones
turn to raging phlox.

Choral

Whinnied by flint,
in the dream-gait that cantered you across
the clover-swarmed
militant field:

this bit
of earth that inches up
to us again, shattered
by the shrill, fife-sharp tone
that jousts you open, million-fold,
in your utmost
heretic word.

Slowly,
you dip your finger into the wound
from which my voice
escapes.

Meridian

All summer long,
by the gradient rasp-light
of our dark, dune-begetting hands: your stones,
crumbling back to life
around you.

Behind my sheer, raven lid,
one early star,
flushed from a hell of briars,
rears you up, innocent,
towards morning, and peoples your shadow
with names.

Night-rhymed. Harrow-deep.
Near.

Lackawanna

Scree-rails, rust,
remembrance: the no longer bearable, again,
shunting across
your gun-metal earth. The eye
does not will
what enters it: it must always refuse
to refuse.

In the burgeoning frost
of equinox: you will have your name,
and nothing more. Dwarfed
to the reddening seed-space
in which every act
rebuts you, your hot, image-bright pore
again
will force its way

open.

Lies. Decrees. 1972.

Imagine:
the conscripting word
that camped in the squalor
of his fathom-moaned, unapproachable
heaven
goes on warring
in time.

Imagine:
even now
he does not repent of
his oath, even
now, he stammers back, unwitnessed, to his
resurrected throne.

Imagine:
the murdered ones,
cursed and radiant below him,
usher the knives
of their humbled, birth-marked silence, deep
into the alleyways
of his mouth.

Imagine:
I speak this to you,
from the evening of the first day,
undyingly,
along the short, human fuse
of resistance.

Ecliptic. Les Halles.

You were my absence.
Wherever I breathed, you found me
lying in the word
that spoke its way back
to this place.

Silence
was
in the prowled shambles
and marrow
of a cunning, harlot haste – a hunger
that became
a bed for me,

as though the random
Ezekiel-wrath
I discovered, the 'Live,' and the
'yes, he said to us,
when we were in our blood,
Live,' had merely been your way
of coming near –

as though somewhere,
visible, an arctic stone, as pale
as semen, had been
dripping, fire-phrase by fire-phrase,
from your lips.

Dictum: After Great Distances

Oleander and rose. The rubble
of earth's other air – where the hummingbird
flies in the shadow
of the hawk. And through each wall, the opening
earth of August,
like a stone that cracks
this wall of sun.

Mountains. And then the lights
of the town
beyond the mountain. The town that lies
on the other side
of light.

We dream
that we do not dream. We wake
in the hours of sleep
and sleep through the silence
that stands over us. Summer
keeps its promise
by breaking it.

Fore-shadows

I breathe you.
I becalm you out of me.
I numb you in the reach
of brethren light.
I suckle you
to the dregs of disaster.

The sky pins a vagrant star
on my chest. I see the wind
as witness, the towering night
that lapsed
in a maze of oaks,
the distance.

I haunt you
to the brink of sorrow.
I milk you of strength.
I defy you,
I deify you
to nothing and
to no one,

I become
your necessary and most violent
heir.

Ireland

Turf-spent, moor-abandoned you,
you, the more naked one, bathed in the dark
of the greenly overrun
deep-glen, of the gray bed
my ghost
pilfered from the mouths
of stones – bestow on me the silence
to shoulder the wings of rooks, allow me
to pass through here again
and breathe the rankly dealt-with air
that still traffics in your shame,
give me the right to destroy you
on the tongue that impales
our harvest, the merciless
acres of cold.

Prism

Earth-time, the stones
tick
in hollows of dust, the arable air
wanders far from home, barbed
wire and road
are erased. Spat
out by the burning
fever in our lungs, the Ur-seed
blooms from crystal, our vermilion breath
refracts us
into many. We will not
ever know ourselves
again. Like the light
that moves between the bars
of light
we sometimes called death,
we, too, will have flowered,
even with such
unquenchable flames
as these.

Wall Writing

Nothing less than nothing.

In the night that comes
from nothing,
for no one in the night
that does not come.

And what stands at the edge of whiteness,
invisible
in the eye of the one who speaks.

Or a word.

Come from nowhere
in the night
of the one who does not come.

Or the whiteness of a word,
scratched
into the wall.

Covenant

Throng of eyes,
myriad, at sunken retina depth: the image
of the great, imageless one,
moored within.

Mantis-lunged, we,
the hirelings, alive in juniper and rubble,
broke the flat bread
that went with us, we
were steps, wandered
into blindness, we knew by then
how to breathe ourselves along
to nothing.

Something lost
became
something to be found.
A name,
followed through the dust
of all that veering, did not ever
divulge its sound. The mountain
was the spoor
by which an animal pain
hunted itself home.

All night
I read the braille wounds
on the inner wall
of your cry, and at the brink
of the thick, millenial morning, climbed up
into you again, where all

my bones began
beating and
beating the heart-drum
to shreds.

Hieroglyph

The language of walls.
Or one last word –
cut
from the visible.

May Day. The metamorphosis
of Solomon's-seal
into stone. The just
doom of the uttered
road, unraveled in the swirl
of pollen-memory
and seed. Do not
emerge, Eden. Stay
in the mouths of the lost
who dream you.

Upon thunder and thorn: the furtive air
arms
the lightning-gorse and silence
of each fallow sky
below. Blood Hebrew. Or what
translates
my body's turning back
to an image of earth.

This knife
I hold against your throat.

White

For one who drowned:
this page, as if
thrown out to sea
in a bottle.

So that
even as the sky embarks
into the seeing of earth, an echo
of the earth
might sail toward him,
filled with a memory of rain,
and the sound of the rain
falling on the water.

So that
he will have learned,
in spite of the wave
now sinking from the crest
of mountains, that forty days
and forty nights
have brought no dove
back to us.

Pastoral

In the hinterland of moss and waiting,
so little like the word
that was a waiting as well,
all has been other
than it is, the moss
still waits for you, the word
is a lantern
you carry to the depths
of green, for even the roots
have carried light, and even now
your voice
still travels through the roots, so that
wherever an axe may fall
you, too, shall know that you live.

Incendiary

Flint hours. The dumb sprawl
of stones around us, heart
against heart, we, in the straw
hulk
that festers through the damp
lapse of night.

Nothing left. The cold eye
opens on cold,
as an image of fire
eats
through the word
that struggles in your mouth. The world
is
whatever you leave to it, is only
you
in the world my body
enters: this place
where all is lacking.

Song of Degrees

In the vacant lots
of solstice. In the light
you wagered for the rubble
of awe. Sand heaps:
retched into prayer – the distance
bought
in your name.

You. And then
you again. A footstep
gives ground: what is more
is not more: nothing
has ever been
enough. Tents,
pitched and struck: a ladder
propped
on a pillow of stone: the sheer
aureole rungs
of fire. You,
and then we. The earth
does not ask
for anyone.

So
be it. So much
the better – so many
words,
raked and murmured along
by your bedouin knees, will not
conjure you home. Even
if you crawled from the skin

of your brother,
you would not go beyond
what you breathe: no
angel can cure you
of your name.

Minima. Memory
and mirage. In each place
you stop for air,
we will build a city
around you. Through the star-
mortared wall
that rises in our night, your soul
will not pass
again.

Fire Speech

You veer out. You crumble in.
You stand.

Cradled
by the hour-gong
that beat through the holly
twelve times
more silent than you, something, let
loose by someone,
rescues your name from coal.

You stand
there again, breathing
in the phantom sun
between ice and reverie.

I have come so far for you,
the voice
that echoes back to me
is no longer my own.

Lapsarian

This bit-open earth.
Arbor: in the neigh of branches.
The shallow night, merging
with noon.

I speak to you
of the word that mires in the smell
of here-after.
I speak to you of the fruit
I shoveled up
from below.
I speak to you of speech.

Humus colors. Buried in the rift
till human. The day's
prismatic blessing – divisible
by breath. Starling paths,
snake furrows, seeds. The quick
skewers of flame. What burns
is banished.
Is taken with you.
Is yours.

A man
walks out from the voice
that became me.
He has vanished.
He has eaten

the ripening word
that killed you and
killed you.

He has found himself,
standing in the place
where the eye most terribly holds
its ground.

Late Summer

Borealis flood, and all of night, unleashed
at the eye's diluvian hour. Our bone-
broken will, countering the flow
of stones within our blood: vertigo
from the helium heights
of language.

Tomorrow: a mountain road
lined with gorse. Sunlight
in the fissures of rock. Lessness.
As if we could hold a single breath
to the limit of breath.

There is no promised land.

Heraclitian

All earth, accountable
to greenness, the air's ballast
coal, and the winter
that ignites
the fire of earth, as all air moves
unbrokenly
into the green
moment of ourselves. We know that we are
spoken for. And we know that earth
will never yield
a word
small enough to hold us. For the just word
is only of air, and in the green
ember
of our nether sameness, it brings no fear
but that of life. We therefore
will be named
by all that we are not. And whoever
sees himself
in what is not yet
spoken,
will know what it is
to fear
earth
to the just
measure of himself.

Braille

Legibility of earth. Bone's
clear pelt,
and the swerve of plume-and-weal clouds
in victim air – no longer
to be read.

'When you stop on this road,
the road, from that moment on,
will vanish.'

And you knew, then,
that there were two of us: you knew
that from all this flesh of air, I
had found the place
where one word
was growing wild.

Nine months darker, my mouth bores through
the bright ways
that cross with yours. Nine lives
deeper, the cry is still
the same.

Salvage

Reunion of ash men
and ash women. Sky's wan hub
grown full till anther-round
on the peat slope from which
I saw them. May-green: what was said,
audible in the eye. The words,
mingled with snow, did not
indict the mouth. I drank
the wine they begrudged me. I stood, perhaps,
beside where you
might have been. I dragged
everything
home to the other world.

Autobiography of the Eye

Invisible things, rooted in cold,
and growing toward this light
that vanishes
into each thing
it illumines. Nothing ends. The hour
returns to the beginning
of the hour in which we breathed: as if
there were nothing. As if I could see
nothing
that is not what it is.

At the limit of summer
and its warmth: blue sky, purple hill.
The distance that survives.
A house, built of air, and the flux
of the air in the air.

Like these stones
that crumble back into earth.
Like the sound of my voice
in your mouth.

All Souls

Anonymity and floe: November
by its only name, death-
danced
through the broken speech
of hoe and furrow
down
from the eaves of overwhelming – these
hammer-worshipped
spew-things
cast
into the zones of blood.

A transfusion of darkness,
the generate peace, encroaching
on slaughter.

Life equal to life.

III: 1975–1977

Disappearances

1 Out of solitude, he begins again –

as if it were the last time
that he would breathe,

and therefore it is now

that he breathes for the first time
beyond the grasp
of the singular.

He is alive, and therefore he is nothing
but what drowns in the fathomless hole
of his eye,

and what he sees
is all that he is not: a city

of the undeciphered
event,

and therefore a language of stones,
since he knows that for the whole of life
a stone
will give way to another stone

to make a wall

and that all these stones
will form the monstrous sum

of particulars.

2 It is a wall. And the wall is death.

   Illegible
   scrawl of discontent, in the image

   and after-image of life –

   and the many who are here
   though never born,
   and those who would speak

   to give birth to themselves.

   He will learn the speech of this place.
   And he will learn to hold his tongue.

   For this is his nostalgia: a man.

3   To hear the silence
    that follows the word of oneself. Murmur

    of the least stone

    shaped in the image
    of earth, and those who would speak
    to be nothing

    but the voice that speaks them
    to the air.

    And he will tell
    of each thing he sees in this space,
    and he will tell it to the very wall
    that grows before him:

    and for this, too, there will be a voice,
    although it will not be his.

    Even though he speaks.

    And because he speaks.

4 There are the many – and they are here:

and for each stone he counts among them
he excludes himself,

as if he, too, might begin to breathe
for the first time

in the space that separates him
from himself.

For the wall is a word. And there is no word
he does not count
as a stone in the wall.

Therefore, he begins again,
and at each moment he begins to breathe

he feels there has never been another
time – as if for the time that he lived
he might find himself

in each thing he is not.

What he breathes, therefore,
is time, and he knows now
that if he lives

it is only in what lives

and will continue to live
without him.

5   In the face of the wall –

    he divines the monstrous
    sum of particulars.

    It is nothing.
    And it is all that he is.
    And if he would be nothing, then let him begin
    where he finds himself, and like any other man
    learn the speech of this place.

    For he, too, lives in the silence
    that comes before the word
    of himself.

6 And of each thing he has seen
he will speak –

the blinding
enumeration of stones,
even to the moment of death –

as if for no other reason
than that he speaks.

Therefore, he says I,
and counts himself
in all that he excludes,

which is nothing,

and because he is nothing
he can speak, which is to say
there is no escape

from the word that is born
in the eye. And whether or not
he would say it,

there is no escape.

7 He is alone. And from the moment he begins to
  breathe,

  he is nowhere. Plural death, born

  in the jaws of the singular,

  and the word that would build a wall
  from the innermost stone
  of life.

  For each thing that he speaks of
  he is not –

  and in spite of himself
  he says I, as if he, too, would begin
  to live in all the others

  who are not. For the city is monstrous,
  and its mouth suffers
  no issue

  that does not devour the word
  of oneself.

  Therefore, there are the many,
  and all these many lives
  shaped into the stones
  of a wall,

and he who would begin to breathe
will learn there is nowhere to go
but here.

Therefore, he begins again,

as if it were the last time
he would breathe.

For there is no more time. And it is the end of time

that begins.

Northern Lights

These are the words
that do not survive the world. And to speak them
is to vanish

into the world. Unapproachable
light
that heaves above the earth, kindling
the brief miracle

of the open eye –

and the day that will spread
like a fire of leaves
through the first chill wind
of October

consuming the world

in the plain speech
of desire.

Reminiscence of Home

True north. Vincent's north.
The glimpsed

unland of light. And through each fissure
of earth, the indigo
fields that burn
in a seething wind of stars.

What is locked
in the eye that possessed you
still serves
as an image of home: the barricade
of an empty chair, and the father, absent,
still blooming in his urn
of honesty.

You will close your eyes.
In the eye of the crow who flies before you,
you will watch yourself
leave yourself behind.

Effigies

Eucalyptus roads: a remnant of the pale sky
shuddering in my throat. Through the ballast
drone of summer

the weeds that silence
even your step.

*

The myriad haunts of light.
And each lost thing – a memory

of what has never been. The hills. The impossible
hills

lost in the brilliance of memory

*

As if it were all

still to be born. Deathless in the eye,
where the eye now opens on the noise

of heat: a wasp, a thistle swaying on the prongs

of barbed wire.

*

Snowfall. And in the nethermost
lode of whiteness – a memory
that adds your steps
to the lost.

Endlessly
I would have walked with you.

*

Alba. The immense, alluvial light. The carillon
of clouds at dawn. And the boats
moored in the jetty fog

are invisible. And if they are there

they are invisible.

*

Gnomon

September sun, illusionless. The purple
field awash
in the hours of the first breath. You will not
submit to this light, or close your eyes
to the vigilant
crumbling of light in your eyes.

Firmament of fact. And you,
like everything else
that moves. Parsed seed
and thimble of air. Fissured
cloud and worm: the open-
ended sentence that engulfs you
at the moment I begin
to be silent.

Perhaps, then, a world
that secretes its harvest
in the lungs, a means
of survival by breath
alone. And if nothing,
then let nothing be
the shadow
that walks inside your shadow, the body
that will cast
the first stone, so that even as you walk
away from yourself, you might feel it
hunger toward you, hourly,
across the enormous
vineyards of the living.

Fragment from Cold

Because we go blind
in the day that goes out with us,
and because we have seen our breath
cloud
the mirror of air,
the eye of the air will open
on nothing but the word
we renounce: winter
will have been a place
of ripeness.

We who become the dead
of another life than ours.

Aubade

Not even the sky.
But a memory of sky,
and the blue of the earth
in your lungs.

Earth
less earth: to watch
how the sky will enclose you, grow vast
with the words
you leave unsaid – and nothing
will be lost.

I am your distress, the seam
in the wall
that opens to the wind
and its stammering, storm
in the plural – this other name
you give your world: exile
in the rooms of home.

Dawn folds, fathers
witness,
the aspen and the ash
that fall. I come back to you
through this fire, a remnant
of the season to come,
and will be to you
as dust, as air,
as nothing

that will not haunt you.
In the place before breath
we feel our shadows cross.

Transfusion

Oven's glow. Or vast
hemoglobin
leap –

:the blasphemy
of their death-devoted word, lying
in the self-same blood
your open heart
still squanders.

Pulse –
and then what – (then
what?) – erupts in the skull
of the ghetto sphinx – that plumbs
the filth
and fever of the ones
who gave up. (Like you,
they still hover, still
hunger, immured in the bread
of no one's flesh, still make themselves
felt):

as if, in the distance between
sundown and sunrise,
a hand
had gathered up your soul
and worked it with the stones
into the leaven
of earth.

Siberian

Shadow, carted off by wolves,
and quartered, half a life beyond
each barb of the wire, now I see you,
magnetic
polar felon, now I begin
to speak to you
of the wild boar
of southern woods, of scrub
oak and thicket spruce, of thyme-reek
and lavender, even
down to lava, spewn, through each
chink in the wall, so that you, counter-voice, lost
in the cold
of farthest murder, might come
floating back
on your barge of ice, bearing
the untellable
cargo of forgiveness.

Clandestine

Remember with me today – the word
and counter-word
of witness: the tactile dawn, emerging
from my clenched hand: sun's
ciliary grasp: the stretch of darkness
I wrote
on the table of sleep.

Now
is the time to come.
All you have come
to take from me, take
away from me now. Do not
forget
to forget. Fill
your pockets with earth,
and seal up the mouth
of my cave.

It was there
I dreamed my life
into a dream
of fire.

Quarry

No more than the song of it. As if
the singing alone
had led us back to this place.

We have been here, and we have never been here.
We have been on the way to where we began,
and we have been lost.

There are no boundaries
in the light. And the earth
leaves no word for us
to sing. For the crumbling of the earth
underfoot

is a music in itself, and to walk among these stones
is to hear nothing
but ourselves.

I sing, therefore, of nothing,

as if it were the place
I do not return to –

and if I should return, then count out my life
in these stones: forget
I was ever here. The world
that walks inside me

is a world beyond reach.

IV: 1978–1979

White Spaces

Something happens, and from the moment it begins to happen, nothing can ever be the same again.

Something happens. Or else, something does not happen. A body moves. Or else, it does not move. And if it moves, something begins to happen. And even if it does not move, something begins to happen.

It comes from my voice. But that does not mean these words will ever be what happens. It comes and goes. If I happen to be speaking at this moment, it is only because I hope to find a way of going along, of running parallel to everything else that is going along, and so begin to find a way of filling the silence without breaking it.

I ask whoever is listening to this voice to forget the words it is speaking. It is important that no one listen too carefully. I want these words to vanish, so to speak, into the silence they came from, and for nothing to remain but a memory of their presence, a token of the fact that they were once here and are here no longer and that during their brief life they seemed not so much to be saying any particular thing as to be the thing that was happening at the same time a certain body was moving in a certain space, that they moved along with everything else that moved.

Something begins, and already it is no longer the beginning, but something else, propelling us into the heart of the thing that is happening. If we were suddenly to stop and ask ourselves, 'Where are we going?', or 'Where are we now?', we would be lost, for at each moment we are no longer where we were, but have left ourselves behind, irrevocably, in a past that has no memory, a past endlessly obliterated by a motion that carries us into the present.

It will not do, then, to ask questions. For this is a landscape of random impulse, of knowledge for its own sake – which is to say, a knowledge that exists, that comes into being beyond any possibility of putting it into words. And if just this once we were to abandon ourselves to the supreme indifference of simply being wherever we happen to be, then perhaps we would not be deluding ourselves into thinking that we, too, had at last become a part of it all.

To think of motion not merely as a function of the body but as an extension of the mind. In the same way, to think of speech not as an extension of the mind but as a function of the body. Sounds emerge from the voice to enter the air and surround and bounce off and enter the body that occupies that air, and though they cannot be seen, these sounds are no less a gesture than a hand is when outstretched in the air towards another hand, and in this gesture can be read the entire alphabet of desire, the body's need to be taken beyond itself, even as it dwells in the sphere of its own motion.

On the surface, this motion seems to be random. But such randomness does not, in itself, preclude a meaning. Or if meaning is not quite the word for it, then say the drift, or a consistent sense of what is happening, even as it changes, moment by moment. To describe it in all its details is probably not impossible. But so many words would be needed, so many streams of syllables, sentences, and subordinate clauses, that the words would always lag behind what was happening, and long after all motion had stopped and each of its witnesses had dispersed, the voice describing that motion would still be speaking, alone, heard by no one, deep into the silence and darkness of these four walls. And yet something is happening, and in spite of myself I want to be present inside the space of this moment, of these moments, and to say something, even though it will be forgotten, that will form a part of this journey for the length of the time it endures.

In the realm of the naked eye nothing happens that does not have its beginning and its end. And yet nowhere can we find the place or the moment at which we can say, beyond a shadow of a doubt, that this is where it begins, or this is where it ends. For some of us, it has begun before the beginning, and for others of us it will go on happening after the end. Where to find it? Don't look. Either it is here or it is not here. And whoever tries to find refuge in any one place, in any one moment, will never be where he thinks he is. In other words, say your goodbyes. It is never too late. It is always too late.

To say the simplest thing possible. To go no farther than whatever it is I happen to find before me. To begin with this landscape, for example. Or even to note the things that are most near, as if in the tiny world before my eyes I might find an image of the life that exists beyond me, as if in a way I do not fully understand each thing in my life were connected to every other thing, which in turn connected me to the world at large, the endless world that looms up in the mind, as lethal and unknowable as desire itself.

To put it another way. It is sometimes necessary not to name the thing we are talking about. The invisible God of the Hebrews, for example, had an unpronounceable name, and each of the ninety-nine names tradition ascribes to this God was in fact nothing more than a way of acknowledging that-which-cannot-be-spoken, that-which-cannot-be-seen, and that-which-cannot-be-understood. But even on a less exalted plane, in the realm of the visible itself, we often hold back from divulging the thing we are talking about. Consider the word 'it'. 'It' is raining, we say, or how is 'it' going? We feel we know what we are saying, and what we mean to say is that it, the word 'it', stands for something that need not be said, or something that cannot be said. But if the thing we say is something that eludes us, something we do not understand, how can we persist in saying that we understand what we are saying? And yet it goes without saying that we do. The 'it', for example, in the preceding sentence, 'it goes without saying', is in fact nothing less than whatever it is that propels us into the act of speech itself. And if it, the word 'it', is what continually recurs in any effort to define it, then it must be accepted as the given, the precondition of the saying of it. It has been said, for example, that words falsify the thing they attempt to say, but even to say 'they falsify' is to admit that 'they falsify' is true, thus betraying an implicit faith in the power of words to say what they mean to say. And yet, when we speak, we often do not mean to say anything, as in the present case, in which I find these words falling from my mouth and vanishing into the silence they came from. In other words, it says itself, and our mouths are merely the instruments of the saying of it. How does it happen? But never do we ask what 'it' happens to be. We know, even if we cannot put it into words. And the feeling that remains within us, the discretion of a knowledge so fully in tune with the world, has no need of whatever it is that might fall from our mouths. Our hearts know what is in them, even if our mouths remain silent. And the world will know what it is, even when nothing remains in our hearts.

A man sets out on a journey to a place he has never been before. Another man comes back. A man comes to a place that has no name, that has no landmarks to tell him where he is. Another man decides to come back. A man writes letters from nowhere, from the white space that has opened up in his mind. The letters are never received. The letters are never sent. Another man sets out on a journey in search of the first man. This second man becomes more and more like the first man, until he, too, is swallowed up by the whiteness. A third man sets out on a journey with no hope of ever getting anywhere. He wanders. He continues to wander. For as long as he remains in the realm of the naked eye, he continues to wander.

I remain in the room in which I am writing this. I put one foot in front of the other. I put one word in front of the other, and for each step I take I add another word, as if for each word to be spoken there were another space to be crossed, a distance to be filled by my body as it moves through this space. It is a journey through space, even if I get nowhere, even if I end up in the same place I started. It is a journey through space, as if into many cities and out of them, as if across deserts, as if to the edge of some imaginary ocean, where each thought drowns in the relentless waves of the real.

I put one foot in front of the other, and then I put the other foot in front of the first, which has now become the other and which will again become the first. I walk within these four walls, and for as long as I am here I can go anywhere I like. I can go from one end of the room to the other and touch any of the four walls, or even all the walls, one after the other, exactly as I like. If the spirit moves me, I can stand in the center of the room. If the spirit moves me in another direction, I can stand in any one of the four corners. Sometimes I touch one of those four corners and in this way bring myself into contact with two walls at the same time. Now and then I let my eyes roam up to the ceiling, and when I am particularly exhausted by my efforts there is always the floor to welcome my body. The light, streaming through the windows, never casts the same shadow twice, and at any given moment I feel myself on the brink of discovering some terrible, unimagined truth. These are moments of great happiness for me.

Somewhere, as if unseen, and yet closer to us than we realize (down the street, for example, or in the next neighborhood), someone is being born. Somewhere else, a car is speeding along an empty highway in the middle of the night. In that same night, a man is hammering a nail into a board. We know nothing about any of this. A seed stirs invisibly in the earth, and we know nothing about it. Flowers wilt, buildings go up, children cry. And yet, for all that, we know nothing.

It happens, and as it continues to happen, we forget where we were when we began. Later, when we have traveled from this moment as far as we have traveled from the beginning, we will forget where we are now. Eventually, we will all go home, and if there are those among us who do not have a home, it is certain, nevertheless, that they will leave this place to go wherever it is they must. If nothing else, life has taught us all this one thing: whoever is here now will not be here later.

I dedicate these words to the things in life I do not understand, to each thing passing away before my eyes. I dedicate these words to the impossibility of finding a word equal to the silence inside me.

In the beginning, I wanted to speak of arms and legs, of jumping up and down, of bodies tumbling and spinning, of enormous journeys through space, of cities, of deserts, of mountain ranges stretching farther than the eye can see. Little by little, however, as these words began to impose themselves on me, the things I wanted to do seemed finally to be of no importance. Reluctantly, I abandoned all my witty stories, all my adventures of far-away places, and began, slowly and painfully, to empty my mind. Now emptiness is all that remains: a space, no matter how small, in which whatever is happening can be allowed to happen.

And no matter how small, each and every possibility remains. Even a motion reduced to an apparent absence of motion. A motion, for example, as minimal as breathing itself, the motion the body makes when inhaling and exhaling air. In a book I once read by Peter Freuchen, the famous Arctic explorer describes being trapped by a blizzard in northern Greenland. Alone, his supplies dwindling, he decided to build an igloo and wait out the storm. Many days passed. Afraid, above all, that he would be attacked by wolves – for he heard them prowling hungrily on the roof of his igloo – he would periodically step outside and sing at the top of his lungs in order to frighten them away. But the wind was blowing fiercely, and no matter how hard he sang, the only thing he could hear was the wind. If this was a serious problem, however, the problem of the igloo itself was much greater. For Freuchen began to notice that the walls of his little shelter were gradually closing in on him. Because of the particular weather conditions outside, his breath was literally freezing to the walls, and with each breath the walls became that much thicker, the igloo became that much smaller, until eventually there was almost no room left for his body. It is surely a frightening thing, to imagine breathing yourself into a coffin of ice, and to my mind considerably more compelling than, say, *The Pit and the Pendulum* by Poe. For in this case it is the man himself who is the agent of his own destruction, and further, the instrument of that destruction is the very thing he needs to keep himself alive. For surely a man cannot live if he does not breathe. But at the same time, he will not live if he does breathe. Curiously, I do not remember how Freuchen managed to escape his predicament. But needless to say, he did escape. The title of the book, if I recall, is *Arctic Adventure*. It has been out of print for many years.

Nothing happens. And still, it is not nothing. To invoke things that have never happened is noble, but how much sweeter to remain in the realm of the naked eye.

It comes down to this: that everything should count, that everything should be a part of it, even the things I do not or cannot understand. The desire, for example, to destroy everything I have written so far. Not from any revulsion at the inadequacy of these words (although that remains a distinct possibility), but rather from the need to remind myself, at each moment, that things do not have to happen this way, that there is always another way, neither better nor worse, in which things might take shape. I realize in the end that I am probably powerless to affect the outcome of even the least thing that happens, but nevertheless, and in spite of myself, as if in an act of blind faith, I want to assume full responsibility. And therefore this desire, this overwhelming need, to take these papers and scatter them across the room. Or else, to go on. Or else, to begin again. Or else, to go on, as if each moment were the beginning, as if each word were the beginning of another silence, another word more silent than the last.

A few scraps of paper. A last cigarette before turning in. The snow falling endlessly in the winter night. To remain in the realm of the naked eye, as happy as I am at this moment. And if this is too much to ask, then to be granted the memory of it, a way of returning to it in the darkness of the night that will surely engulf me again. Never to be anywhere but here. And the immense journey through space that continues. Everywhere, as if each place were here. And the snow falling endlessly in the winter night.

Credo

The infinite

tiny things. For once merely to breathe
in the light of the infinite

tiny things
that surround us. Or nothing
can escape

the lure of this darkness, the eye
will discover that we are
only what has made us less
than we are. To say nothing. To say:
our very lives

depend on it.

Obituary in the Present Tense

It is all one to him –
where he begins

and where he ends. Egg white, the white
of his eye: he says
bird milk, sperm

sliding from the word
of himself. For the eye
is evanescent,
clings only to what is, no more here

or less there, but everywhere, every

thing. He memorizes
none of it. Nor does he write

anything down. He abstains
from the heart

of living things. He waits.

And if he begins, he will end,
as if his eye had opened in the mouth

of a bird, as if he had never begun

to be anywhere. He speaks
from distances
no less far than these.

Narrative

Because what happens will never happen,
and because what has happened
endlessly happens again,

we are as we were, everything
has changed in us, if we speak
of the world
it is only to leave the world

unsaid. Early winter: the yellow apples still
unfallen
in a naked tree, the tracks
of invisible deer

in the first snow, and then the snow
that does not stop. We repent
of nothing. As if we could stand
in this light. As if we could stand in the silence
of this single moment

of light.

S. A. 1911–1979

From loss. And from such loss
that marauds the mind – even to the loss

of mind. To begin with this thought: without rhyme

or reason. And then simply to wait. As if the first
    word
comes only after the last, after a life
of waiting for the word

that was lost. To say no more
than the truth of it: men die, the world fails, the
    words

have no meaning. And therefore to ask
only for words.

Stone wall. Stone heart. Flesh and blood.

As much as all this.
More.

Search for a Definition
(On Seeing a Painting by Bradley Walker Tomlin)

Always the smallest act

possible
in this time of acts

larger than life, a gesture
toward the thing that passes

almost unseen. A small wind

disturbing a bonfire, for example,
which I found the other day
by accident

on a museum wall. Almost nothing
is there: a few wisps
of white

thrown idly against the pure black
background, no more
than a small gesture
trying to be nothing

more than itself. And yet
it is not here
and to my eyes will never become
a question
of trying to simplify

the world, but a way of looking for a place
to enter the world, a way of being
present
among the things
that do not want us – but which we need
to the same measure that we need
ourselves. Only a moment before
the beautiful

woman
who stood before me
had been saying how much she wanted
a child
and how time was beginning
to run out on her. We said
we must each write a poem
using the words 'a small
wind

disturbing a bonfire'. Since that time
nothing

has meant more than the small
act
present in these words, the act
of trying to speak

words

that mean almost nothing. To the very end
I want to be equal
to whatever it is
my eye will bring me, as if
I might finally see myself

let go
in the nearly invisible
things

that carry us along with ourselves and all
the unborn children

into the world.

Between the Lines

Stone-pillowed, the ways
of remoteness. And written in your palm,
the road.

Home, then, is not home
but the distance between
blessed
and unblessed. And whoever puts himself
into the skin
of his brother, will know
what sorrow is
to the seventh year
beyond the seventh year
of the seventh year.

And divide his children in half.

And wrestle in darkness
with an angel.

In Memory of Myself

Simply to have stopped.

As if I could begin
where my voice has stopped, myself
the sound of a word

I cannot speak.

So much silence
to be brought to life
in this pensive flesh, the beating
drum of words
within, so many words

lost in the wide world
within me, and thereby to have known
that in spite of myself

I am here.

As if this were the world.

Bedrock

Dawn as an image
of dawn, and the very sky collapsing
into itself. Irreducible

image
of pure water, the pores of earth
exuding light: such yield

as only light will bring, and the very stones
undead

in the image of themselves.

The consolation of color.

Facing the Music

Blue. And within that blue a feeling
of green, the gray blocks of clouds
buttressed against air, as if
in the idea of rain
the eye
could master the speech
of any given moment

on earth. Call it the sky. And so
to describe
whatever it is
we see, as if it were nothing
but the idea
of something we had lost
within. For we can begin
to remember

the hard earth, the flint
reflecting stars, the undulating
oaks set loose
by the heaving of air, and so down
to the least seed, revealing what grows
above us, as if
because of this blue there could be
this green

that spreads, myriad
and miraculous
in this, the most silent
moment of summer. Seeds
speak of this juncture, define

where the air and the earth erupt
in this profusion of chance, the random
forces of our own lack
of knowing what it is
we see, and merely to speak of it
is to see
how words fail us, how nothing comes right
in the saying of it, not even these words
I am moved to speak
in the name of this blue
and green
that vanish into the air
of summer.

      Impossible
to hear it anymore. The tongue
is forever taking us away
from where we are, and nowhere
can we be at rest
in the things we are given
to see, for each word
is an elsewhere, a thing that moves
more quickly than the eye, even
as this sparrow moves, veering
into the air
in which it has no home. I believe, then,
in nothing

these words might give you, and still
I can feel them
speaking through me, as if
this alone
is what I desire, this blue
and this green, and to say
how this blue
has become for me the essence
of this green, and more than the pure

seeing of it, I want you to feel
this word
that has lived inside me
all day long, this
desire for nothing

but the day itself, and how it has grown
inside my eyes, stronger
than the word it is made of, as if
there could never be another word

that would hold me
without breaking.

Essays

The Art of Hunger

> What is important, it seems to me, is not so much to defend a culture whose existence has never kept a man from going hungry, as to extract, from what is called culture, ideas whose compelling force is identical with that of hunger.
>
> *Antonin Artaud*

A young man comes to a city. He has no name, no home, no work: he has come to the city to write. He writes. Or, more exactly, he does not write. He starves to the point of death.

The city is Christiania (Oslo); the year is 1890. The young man wanders through the streets: the city is a labyrinth of hunger, and all his days are the same. He writes unsolicited articles for a local paper. He worries about his rent, his disintegrating clothes, the difficulty of finding his next meal. He suffers. He nearly goes mad. He is never more than one step from collapse.

Still, he writes. Now and then he manages to sell an article, to find a temporary reprieve from his misery. But he is too weak to write steadily and can rarely finish the pieces he has begun. Among his abortive works are an essay entitled 'Crimes of the Future', a philosophical tract on the freedom of the will, an allegory about a bookstore fire (the books are brains), and a play set in the Middle Ages, 'The Sign of the Cross'. The process is inescapable: he must eat in order to write. But if he does not write, he will not eat. And if he cannot eat, he cannot write. He cannot write.

He writes. He does not write. He wanders through the streets of the city. He talks to himself in public. He frightens people away from him. When, by chance, he comes into some money, he gives it away. He is evicted from his room. He eats, and then throws everything up. At one point, he has a brief flirtation with a girl, but nothing comes of it except humiliation. He hungers. He curses the world. He does not die. In the end, for no apparent reason, he signs on board a ship and leaves the city.

These are the bare bones of Knut Hamsun's first novel, *Hunger*. It is a work devoid of plot, action, and – but for the narrator – character. By nineteenth-century standards, it is a work in which nothing happens. The radical subjectivity of the narrator effectively eliminates the basic concerns of the traditional novel. Similar to the hero's plan to make an 'invisible detour' when he came to the problem of space and time in one of his essays, Hamsun manages to dispense with historical time, the basic organizing principle of nineteenth-century fiction. He gives us an account only of the hero's worst struggles with hunger. Other, less difficult times, in which his hunger has been appeased – even though they might last as long as a week – are passed off in one or two sentences. Historical time is obliterated in favor of inner duration. With only an arbitrary beginning and an arbitrary ending, the novel faithfully records the vagaries of the narrator's mind, following each thought from its mysterious inception through all its meanderings, until it dissipates and the next thought begins. What happens is allowed to happen.

This novel cannot even claim to have a redeeming social value. Although *Hunger* puts us in the jaws of misery, it offers no analysis of that misery, contains no call to political action. Hamsun, who turned fascist in his old age during the Second World War, never concerned himself with the problems of class injustice, and his narrator-hero, like Dostoevsky's Raskolnikov, is not so much an underdog as a monster of intellectual arrogance. Pity plays no part in *Hunger*. The hero suffers, but only because he has chosen to suffer. Hamsun's art is such that he rigorously prevents us from feeling any compassion for his character. From the very beginning, it is made clear that the hero need not starve. Solutions exist, if not in the city, then at least in departure. But buoyed by an obsessive, suicidal pride, the young man's actions continually betray a scorn for his own best interests.

> I began running so as to punish myself, left street after street behind me, pushed myself on with inward jeers, and screeched silently and furiously at myself whenever I felt like stopping. With the help of these exertions I ended up along Pile Street. When I finally did stop, almost weeping with anger that I couldn't run any farther, my whole body trembled, and I threw myself down on a house stoop. 'Not so fast!' I said. And to torture myself right, I stood up again and forced myself to stand there, laughing at myself and gloating over my own fatigue. Finally, after a few minutes, I nodded and so gave myself permission to sit down; however, I chose the most uncomfortable spot on the stoop.*

He seeks out what is most difficult in himself, courting pain and adversity in the same way other men seek out pleasure. He goes hungry, not because he has to, but from some inner compulsion, as if to wage a hunger strike against himself. Before the book begins, before the reader has been made the privileged witness of his fate, the hero's course of action has been fixed. A process is already in motion, and although the hero cannot control it, that does not mean he is unaware of what he is doing.

> I was conscious all the time that I was following mad whims without being able to do anything about it . . . Despite my alienation from myself at that moment, and even though I was nothing but a battleground for invisible forces, I was aware of every detail of what was going on around me.

Having withdrawn into a nearly perfect solitude, he has become both the subject and object of his own experiment.

---

*All quotations are from the Robert Bly translation, Farrar, Straus, and Giroux, 1967.

Hunger is the means by which this split takes place, the catalyst, so to speak, of altered consciousness.

> I had noticed very clearly that every time I went hungry a little too long it was as though my brains simply ran quietly out of my head and left me empty. My head became light and floating, I could no longer feel its weight upon my shoulders . . .

If it is an experiment, however, it has nothing to do with the scientific method. There are no controls, no stable points of reference – only variables. Nor can this separation of mind and body be reduced to a philosophical abstraction. We are not in the realm of ideas here. It is a physical state, brought into being under conditions of extreme duress. Mind and body have been weakened; the hero has lost control over both his thoughts and actions. And yet he persists in trying to control his destiny. This is the paradox, the game of circular logic that is played out through the pages of the book. It is an impossible situation for the hero. For he has willfully brought himself to the brink of danger. To give up starving would not mean victory, it would simply mean that the game was over. He wants to survive, but only on his own terms: survival that will bring him face to face with death.

He fasts. But not in the way a Christian would fast. He is not denying earthly life in anticipation of heavenly life; he is simply refusing to live the life he has been given. And the longer he goes on with his fast, the more death intrudes itself upon his life. He approaches death, creeps towards the edge of the abyss, and once there, clings to it, unable to move either forward or backward. Hunger, which opens the void, does not have the power to seal it up. A brief moment of Pascalian terror has been transformed into a permanent condition.

His fast, then, is a contradiction. To persist in it would mean death, and with death the fast would end. He must therefore stay alive, but only to the extent that it keeps him on the point of death. The idea of ending is resisted in the interests of maintaining the constant possibility of the end. Because his fasting neither posits a goal nor offers a promise of redemption, its contradiction must remain unresolved. As such, it is an image of despair, generated by the same self-consuming passion as the sickness unto death. The soul, in its despair, seeks to devour itself, and because it cannot – precisely because it despairs – sinks further into despair.

Unlike a religious art, in which self-debasement can play an ultimately cleansing role (the meditative poetry of the seventeenth century, for example), hunger only simulates the dialectic of salvation. In Fulke Greville's poem, 'Down in the depth of mine iniquity', the poet is able to look into a 'fatal mirror of transgression' which 'shows man as fruit of his degeneration', but he knows that this is only the first step in a two-fold process, for it is in this mirror that Christ is revealed 'for the same sins dying / And from that hell I feared, to free me, come . . .' In Hamsun's novel, however, once the depths have been sounded, the mirror of meditation remains empty.

He remains at the bottom, and no God will come to rescue the young man. He cannot even depend on the props of social convention to keep him standing. He is rootless, without friends, denuded of objects. Order has disappeared for him; everything has become random. His actions are inspired by nothing but whim and ungovernable urge, the weary frustration of anarchic discontent. He pawns his waistcoat in order to give alms to a beggar, hires a carriage in search of a fictitious acquaintance, knocks on strangers' doors, and repeatedly asks the time of passing policemen, for the single reason that he fancies to do so. He does not revel in these actions, however. They remain profoundly disquieting for him. Furiously trying to stabilize his life, to put an end to his wanderings, find a room, and settle down to his writing, he is thwarted by the fast he has set in motion. Once it starts, hunger does not release its progenitor-victim until its lesson has been made unforgettable. The hero is seized against his will by a force of his own making and is compelled to respond to its demands.

He loses everything – even himself. Reach the bottom of a Godless hell, and identity disappears. It is no accident that Hamsun's hero has no name: as time goes on, he is truly shorn of his self. What names he chooses to give himself are all inventions, summoned forth on the spur of the moment. He cannot say who he is because he does not know. His name is a lie, and with this lie the reality of his world vanishes.

He peers into the darkness hunger has created for him, and what he finds is a void of language. Reality has become a confusion of thingless names and nameless things for him. The connection between self and world has been broken.

> I remained for a while looking into the dark – this dense substance of darkness that had no bottom, which I couldn't understand. My thoughts could not grasp such a thing. It seemed to be a dark beyond all measurement, and I felt its presence weight me down. I closed my eyes and took to singing half aloud and rocking myself back and forth on the cot to amuse myself, but it did no good. The dark had captured my brain and gave me not an instant of peace. What if I myself became dissolved into the dark, turned into it?

At the precise moment that he is in the greatest fear of losing possession of himself, he suddenly imagines that he has invented a new word: *Kubooa* – a word in no language, a word with no meaning.

> I had arrived at the joyful insanity hunger was: I was empty and free of pain, and my thoughts no longer had any check.

He tries to think of a meaning for his word but can only come up with what it doesn't mean, which is neither 'God', nor the 'Tivoli Gardens', nor 'cattle show', nor 'padlock', nor 'sunrise', nor 'emigration', nor 'tobacco factory', nor 'yarn'.

No, the word was actually intended to mean something spiritual, a feeling, a state of mind – if only I could understand it? And I thought and thought to find something spiritual.

But he does not succeed. Voices, not his own, begin to intrude, to confuse him, and he sinks deeper into chaos. After a violent fit, in which he imagines himself to be dying, all goes still, with no sounds but those of his own voice, rolling back from the wall.

This episode is perhaps the most painful in the book. But it is only one of many examples of the hero's language disease. Throughout the narrative, his pranks most often take the form of lies. Retrieving his lost pencil from a pawn shop (he had accidentally left it in the pocket of a vest he had sold), he tells the proprietor that it was with this very pencil that he had written his three-volume treatise on Philosophical Consciousness. An insignificant pencil, he admits, but he has a sentimental attachment to it. To an old man on a park bench he recites the fantastic story of a Mr Happolati, the inventor of the electric prayer book. Asking a store clerk to wrap his last possession, a tattered green blanket that he is too ashamed to carry around exposed to view, he explains that it is not really the blanket he wants wrapped, but the pair of priceless vases he has folded inside the blanket. Not even the girl he courts is immune from this sort of fiction. He invents a name for her, a name that pleases him for its beauty, and he refuses to call her by anything else.

These lies have a meaning beyond the jests of the moment. In the realm of language the lie has the same relationship to truth that evil has to good in the realm of morals. That is the convention, and it works if we believe in it. But Hamsun's hero no longer believes in anything. Lies and truths are as one to him. Hunger has led him into the darkness, and there is no turning back.

This equation of language and morals becomes the gist of the final episode in *Hunger*.

My brain grew clearer, I understood that I was close to total collapse. I put my hands against the wall and shoved to push myself away from it. The street was still dancing around. I began to hiccup from fury, and struggled with every bit of energy against my collapse, fought a really stout battle not to fall down. I didn't want to fall, I wanted to die standing. A wholesale grocer's cart came by and I saw it was filled with potatoes, but out of fury, from sheer obstinacy, I decided that they were not potatoes at all, they were cabbages, and I swore violent oaths that they were cabbages. I heard my own words very well, and I took the oath again and again on this lie, and swore deliberately just to have the delightful satisfaction of committing such clear perjury. I became drunk over this superb sin, I lifted three fingers in the air and swore with trembling lips in the name of the Father, the Son, and the Holy Ghost that they were cabbages.

And that is the end of it. There are only two possibilities left for the hero now: live or die; and he chooses to live. He has said no to society, no to God, no to his own words. Later that same day he leaves the city. There is no longer any need to continue the fast. Its work has been done.

Hunger: or a portrait of the artist as a young man. But it is an apprenticeship that has little in common with the early struggles of other writers. Hamsun's hero is no Stephen Dedalus, and there is hardly a word in *Hunger* about aesthetic theory. The world of art has been translated into the world of the body – and the original text has been abandoned. Hunger is not a metaphor; it is the very crux of the problem itself. If others, such as Rimbaud, with his program for the voluntary derangement of the senses, have turned the body into an aesthetic principle in its own right, Hamsun's hero steadfastly rejects the opportunity to use his deficiencies to his own advantage. He is weak, he has lost control over his thoughts, and yet he continues to strive for lucidity in his writing. But hunger affects his prose in the same way it affects his life. Although he is willing to sacrifice everything for his art, even submit to the worst forms of debasement and misery, all he has really done is make it impossible for himself to write. You cannot write on an empty stomach, no matter how hard you try. But it would be wrong to dismiss the hero of *Hunger* as a fool or a madman. In spite of the evidence, he knows what he is doing. He does not want to succeed. He wants to fail.

Something new is happening here, some new thought about the nature of art is being proposed in *Hunger*. It is first of all an art that is indistinguishable from the life of the artist who makes it. That is not to say an art of autobiographical excess, but rather, an art that is the direct expression of the effort to express itself. In other words, an art of hunger: an art of need, of necessity, of desire. Certainty yields to doubt, form gives way to process. There can be no arbitrary imposition of order, and yet, more than ever, there is the obligation to achieve clarity. It is an art that begins with the knowledge that there are no right answers. For that reason, it becomes essential to ask the right questions. One finds them by living them. To quote Samuel Beckett:

> What I am saying does not mean that there will henceforth be no form in art. It only means that there will be a new form, and that this form will be of such a type that it admits the chaos and does not try to say that the chaos is really something else . . . To find a form that accommodates the mess, that is the task of the artist now.*

Hamsun gives the portrait of this artist in the first stages of his development. But it is in Kafka's story, *A Hunger Artist*, that the aesthetics of hunger receives its most meticulous elaboration. Here the contradictions of the fast conducted by Hamsun's hero – and the artistic impasse it leads to – are

---

*From an interview with Tom Driver, 'Beckett at the Madeleine', in *The Columbia University Forum*, Summer 1961.

joined in a parable that deals with an artist whose art consists in fasting. The hunger artist is at once an artist and not an artist. Though he wants his performances to be admired, he insists that they shouldn't be admired, because they have nothing to do with art. He has chosen to fast only because he could never find any food that he liked. His performances are therefore not spectacles for the amusement of others, but the unravelling of a private despair that he has permitted others to watch.

Like Hamsun's hero, the hunger artist has lost control over himself. Beyond the theatrical device of sitting in his cage, his art in no way differs from his life, even what his life would have been had he not become a performer. He is not trying to please anyone. In fact, his performances cannot even be understood or appreciated.

> No one could possibly watch the hunger artist continuously, day and night, and so no one could produce first hand evidence that the fast had really been rigorous and continuous; only the artist himself could know that; he was therefore bound to be the sole completely satisfied spectator of his own fast.

This is not the classic story of the misunderstood artist, however. For the very nature of the fast resists comprehension. Knowing itself from the outset to be an impossibility, and condemning itself to certain failure, it is a process that moves asymptotically towards death, destined to reach neither fruition nor destruction. In Kafka's story, the hunger artist dies, but only because he forsakes his art, abandoning the restrictions that had been imposed on him by his manager. The hunger artist goes too far. But that is the risk, the danger inherent in any act of art: you must be willing to give your life.

In the end, the art of hunger can be described as an existential art. It is a way of looking death in the face, and by death I mean death as we live it today: without God, without hope of salvation. Death as the abrupt and absurd end of life.

I do not believe that we have come any farther than this. It is even possible that we have been here much longer than we are willing to admit. In all this time, however, only a few artists have been able to recognize it. It takes courage, and not many of us would be willing to risk everything for nothing. But that is what happens in *Hunger*, a novel written in 1890. Hamsun's character systematically unburdens himself of every belief in every system, and in the end, by means of the hunger he has inflicted upon himself, he arrives at nothing. There is nothing to keep him going – and yet he keeps on going. He walks straight into the twentieth century.

1970

Pages for Kafka
on the fiftieth anniversary of his death

He wanders toward the promised land. That is to say: he moves from one place to another, and dreams continually of stopping. And because this desire to stop is what haunts him, is what counts most for him, he does not stop. He wanders. That is to say: without the slightest hope of ever going anywhere.

He is never going anywhere. And yet he is always going. Invisible to himself, he gives himself up to the drift of his own body, as if he could follow the trail of what refuses to lead him. And by the blindness of the way he has chosen, against himself, in spite of himself, with its veerings, detours, and circlings back, his step, always one step in front of nowhere, invents the road he has taken. It is his road, and his alone. And yet on this road he is never free. For all he has left behind still anchors him to his starting place, makes him regret ever having taken the first step, robs him of all assurance in the rightness of departure. And the farther he travels from his starting place, the greater his doubt grows. His doubt goes with him, like breath, like his breathing between each step – fitful, oppressive – so that no true rhythm, no one pace, can be held. And the farther his doubt goes with him, the nearer he feels to the source of that doubt, so that in the end it is the sheer distance between him and what he has left behind that allows him to see what is behind him: what he is not and might have been. But this thought brings him neither solace nor hope. For the fact remains that he has left all this behind, and in all these things, now consigned to absence, to the longing born of absence, he might once have found himself, fulfilled himself, by following the one law given to him, to remain, and which he now transgresses, by leaving.

All this conspires against him, so that at each moment, even as he continues on his way, he feels he must turn his eyes from the distance that lies before him, like a lure, to the movement of his feet, appearing and disappearing below him, to the road itself, its dust, the stones that clutter its way, the sound of his feet clattering upon them, and he obeys this feeling, as though it were a penance, and he, who would have married the distance before him, becomes, against himself, in spite of himself, the intimate of all that is near. Whatever he can touch, he lingers over, examines, describes with a patience that at each moment exhausts him, overwhelms him, so that even as he goes on, he calls this going into question, and questions each step he is about to take. He who lives for an encounter with the unseen becomes the instrument of the seen: he who would quarry the earth becomes the spokesman of its surfaces, the surveyor of its shades.

Whatever he does, then, he does for the sole purpose of subverting himself, of undermining his strength. If it is a matter of going on, he will do everything in his power not to go on. And yet he will go on. For even though he lingers, he is incapable of rooting himself. No pause conjures a place. But this, too, he knows. For what he wants is what he does not want. And if his journey has any end, it will only be by finding himself, in the end, where he began.

He wanders. On a road that is not a road, on an earth that is not his earth, an exile in his own body. Whatever is given to him, he will refuse. Whatever is spread before him, he will turn his back on. He will refuse, the better to hunger for what he has denied himself. For to enter the promised land is to despair of ever coming near it. Therefore, he holds everything away from him, at arm's length, at life's length, and comes closest to arriving when farthest from his destination. And yet he goes on. And from one step to the next he finds nothing but himself. Not even himself, but the shadow of what he will become. For in the least stone touched, he recognizes a fragment of the promised land. Not even the promised land, but its shadow. And between shadow and shadow lives light. And not just any light, but this light, the light that grows inside him, unendingly, as he goes along his way.

1974

New York Babel

In the preface to his novel *Le Bleu du Ciel*, Georges Bataille makes an important distinction between books that are written for the sake of experiment and books that are born of necessity. Literature, Bataille argues, is an essentially disruptive force, a presence confronted in 'fear and trembling' that is capable of revealing to us the truth of life and its *excessive* possibilities. Literature is not a continuum, but a series of dislocations, and the books that mean most to us in the end are usually those which ran counter to the idea of literature that prevailed at the time they were written. Bataille speaks of 'a moment of *rage*' as the kindling spark of all great works: it cannot be summoned by an act of will, and its source is always extra-literary. 'How can we linger', he says, 'over books we feel the author was not *compelled* to write?' Self-conscious experimentation is generally the result of a real longing to break down the barriers of literary convention. But most avant-garde works do not survive; in spite of themselves, they remain prisoners of the very conventions they try to destroy. The poetry of Futurism, for example, which made such a commotion in its day, is hardly read by anyone now except scholars and historians of the period. On the other hand, certain writers who played little or no part in the literary life around them – Kafka, for example – have gradually come to be recognized as essential. The work that revives our sense of literature, that gives us a new feeling for what literature can be, is the work that changes our life. It often seems improbable, as if it had come from nowhere, and because it stands so ruthlessly outside the norm, we have no choice but to create a new place for it.

Le Schizo et les Langues by Louis Wolfson* is such a book. It is

---

*Published by Editions Gallimard in 1971. Preface by Gilles Deleuze.

not only improbable, but totally unlike anything that has come before it. To say that it is a work written in the margins of literature is not enough: its place, properly speaking, is in the margins of language itself. Written in French by an American, it has little meaning unless it is considered an American book; and yet, for reasons that will be made clear, it is also a book that excludes all possibility of translation. It hovers somewhere in the limbo between the two languages, and nothing will ever be able to rescue it from this precarious existence. For what we are presented with here is not simply the case of a writer who has chosen to write in a foreign language. The author of this book has written in French precisely because he had no choice. It is the result of brute necessity, and the book itself is nothing less than an act of survival.

Louis Wolfson is a schizophrenic. He was born in 1931 and lives in New York. For want of a better description, I would call his book a kind of third-person autobiography, a memoir of the present, in which he records the facts of his disease and the utterly bizarre method he has devised for dealing with it. Referring to himself as 'the schizophrenic student of languages', 'the mentally ill student', 'the demented student of idioms', Wolfson uses a narrative style that partakes of both the dryness of a clinical report and the inventiveness of fiction. Nowhere in the text is there even the slightest trace of delirium or 'madness': every passage is lucid, forthright, objective. As we read along, wandering through the labyrinth of the author's obsessions, we come to feel with him, to identify with him, in the same way we identify with the eccentricities and torments of Kirilov, or Molloy.

Wolfson's problem is the English language, which has become intolerably painful to him, and which he refuses either to speak or listen to. He has been in and out of mental institutions for over ten years, steadfastly resisting all cooperation with the doctors, and now, at the time he is writing the book (the late sixties), he is living in the cramped lower-middle-class apartment of his mother and stepfather. He spends his days sitting at his desk studying foreign languages

– principally French, German, Russian, and Hebrew – and protecting himself against any possible assault of English by keeping his fingers stuck in his ears, or listening to foreign language broadcasts on his transistor radio with two earplugs, or keeping a finger in one ear and an earplug in the other. In spite of these precautions, however, there are times when he is not able to ward off the intrusion of English – when his mother, for example, bursts into his room shrieking something to him in her loud and high-pitched voice. It becomes clear to the student that he cannot drown out English by simply translating it into another language. Converting an English word into its foreign equivalent leaves the English word intact; it has not been destroyed, but only put to the side, and is still there waiting to menace him.

The system that he develops in answer to this problem is complex, but not difficult to follow once one has become familiar with it, since it is based on a consistent set of rules. Drawing on the several languages he has studied, he becomes able to transform English words and phrases into phonetic combinations of foreign letters, syllables, and words that form new linguistic entities, which not only resemble the English in meaning, but in sound as well. His descriptions of these verbal acrobatics are highly detailed, often taking up as many as ten pages, but perhaps the end result of one of the simpler examples will give some idea of the process. The sentence, 'Don't trip over the wire!' is changed in the following manner: 'Don't' becomes the German 'Tu'nicht', 'trip' becomes the first four letters of the French 'trébucher', 'over' becomes the German 'über', 'the' becomes the Hebrew 'èth hé', and 'wire' becomes the German 'zwirn', the middle three letters of which correspond to the first three letters of the English word: 'Tu'nicht tréb über èth hé zwirn.' At the end of this passage, exhausted but gratified by his efforts, Wolfson writes: 'If the schizophrenic did not experience a feeling of joy as a result of his having found, that day, these foreign words to annihilate yet another word of his mother tongue (for perhaps, in fact, he was incapable of this sentiment), he certainly felt much less miserable than usual, at least for a while.'*

The book, however, is far more than just a catalogue of these transformations. They are at the core of the work, and in some sense define its purpose, but the real substance is elsewhere, in the human situation and daily life that envelop Wolfson's preoccupation with language. There are few books that have given a more immediate feeling of what it is like to live in New York and to wander through the streets of the city. Wolfson's eye for detail is excruciatingly precise, and each nuance of his observations – whether it be the prison-like atmosphere of the Forty-Second Street Public Library reading room, the anxieties of a high school dance, the Times Square prostitute scene, or a conversation with his father on a bench in a city park – is rendered with attentiveness and authority. A strange movement of objectification is continually at work, and much of the fascination of the prose is a result of this distancing, which acts as a kind of lure, always drawing us *toward* what is written. By treating himself in the third person, Wolfson is able to create a space between himself and himself, to prove to himself that he exists. The French language serves much the same function. By looking out on his world through a different lens, by punning his world – which is immured in English – into a different language, he is able to see it with new eyes, in a way that is less oppressive to him, as if, to some slight degree, he were able to have an effect upon it.

His powers of evocation are devastating, and in his toneless, deadpan style, he manages to present a portrait of life among the Jewish poor that is so horrendously comical and vivid that it stands comparison with the early passages of Céline's *Death on the Installment Plan*. There seems to be no question that Wolfson knows what he is doing. His aims are not aesthetic ones, but in his patient determination to record everything, to set down the facts as accurately as possible, he has exposed the true absurdity of his situation, which he is

---

*My translation.

often able to respond to with an ironical sense of detachment and whimsy.

His parents were divorced when he was four or five years old. His father has spent most of his life on the periphery of the world, without work, living in cheap hotels, idling away his time in cafeterias smoking cigars. He claims that his marriage took place 'with a cat in the bag', since it was not until later that he learned his wife had a glass eye. When she eventually remarried, her second husband disappeared after the wedding with her diamond ring – only to be tracked down by her and thrown into jail the moment he stepped off a plane a thousand miles away. His release was granted only on the condition that he go back to his wife.

The mother is the dominant, suffocating presence of the book, and when Wolfson speaks of his 'langue maternelle', it is clear that his abhorrence of English is in direct function to his abhorrence of his mother. She is a grotesque character, a monster of vulgarity, who ridicules her son's language studies, insists on speaking to him in English, and perseveres in doing exactly the opposite of what would make his life bearable. She spends much of her spare time playing popular songs on an electric organ, with the volume turned up full blast. Sitting over his books, his fingers stuck in his ears, the student sees the lampshade on his desk begin to rattle, to feel the whole room vibrate in rhythm to the piece, and as soon as the deafening music penetrates him, he automatically thinks of the English lyrics of the songs, which drives him into a fury of despair. (Half a chapter is devoted to his linguistic transformation of the words to *Good Night Ladies*.) But Wolfson never really judges her. He only describes. And if he allows himself an occasional smirk of understatement, it would seem to be his right.

'Naturally, her optical weakness seemed in no way to interfere with the capacity of her speech organs (perhaps it was even the reverse), and she would speak, at least for the most part, in a very high and very shrill voice, even though she was positively able to whisper over the telephone when she wanted to arrange secretly for her son's entrance into the psychiatric hospital, that is to say, without his knowledge.'

Beyond the constant threat of English posed by his mother (who is the very embodiment of the language for him), the student suffers from her in her role as provider. Throughout the book, his linguistic activities are counterpointed by his obsession with food, eating, and the possible contamination of his food. He oscillates between a violent disgust at the thought of eating, as if it were a basic contradiction of his language work, and terrifying orgies of gluttony that leave him sick for hours afterward. Each time he enters the kitchen, he arms himself with a foreign book, repeats aloud certain foreign phrases he has been memorizing, and forces himself to avoid reading the English labels on the packages and cans of food. Reciting one of the phrases over and over again, like a magical incantation to keep away evil spirits, he tears open the first package that comes to hand – containing the food that is easiest to eat, which is usually the least nutritional – and begins to stuff the food into his mouth, all the while making sure that it does not touch his lips, which he feels must be infested with the eggs and larvae of parasites. After such bouts, he is filled with self-recriminations and guilt. As Gilles Deleuze suggests in his preface to the book, 'His guilt is no less great when he has eaten than when he has heard his mother speak. It is the same guilt.'

This is the point, I feel, at which Wolfson's private nightmare locks with certain universal questions about language. There is a fundamental connection between speaking and eating, and by the very excessiveness of Wolfson's experience, we are able to see how profound this relationship is. Speech is a strangeness, an anomaly, a biologically secondary function of the mouth, and myths about language are often linked to the idea of food. Adam is granted the power of naming the creatures of Paradise and is later expelled for having eaten of the Tree of Knowledge. Mystics fast in order to prepare themselves to receive the word of God. The body of Christ, the word made flesh, is eaten in holy communion. It is as if the life-serving function of the mouth, its role in eating, had been transferred to speech, for it is language that creates us and defines us as human beings. Wolfson's fear of eating, the guilt he feels over his escapades of self-indulgence, are an acknowledgement of his betrayal of the task he has set for himself: that of discovering a language he can live with. To eat is a compromise, since it sustains him within the context of an already discredited and unacceptable world.

In the end, Wolfson's search is undertaken in the hope of one day being able to speak English again – a hope that flickers now and then through the pages of the book. The invention of his system of transformations, the writing of the book itself, are part of a slow progression beyond the hermetic agony of his disease. By refusing to allow anyone to impose a cure on him, by forcing himself to confront his own problems, to live through them alone, he senses in himself a dawning awareness of the *possibility* of living among others – of being able to break free from his one-man language and enter a language of men.

The book he has created from this struggle is difficult to define, but it should not be dismissed as a therapeutic exercise, as yet another document of mental illness to be filed on the shelves of medical libraries. Gallimard, it seems to me, has made a serious error in bringing out *Le Schizo et les Langues* as part of a series on psychoanalysis. By giving the book a label, they have somehow tried to tame the rebellion that gives the book its extraordinary force, to soften 'the moment of rage' that everywhere informs Wolfson's writing.

On the other hand, even if we avoid the trap of considering this work as nothing more than a case history, we should still hesitate to judge it by established literary standards and to look for parallels with other literary works. Wolfson's method, in some sense, does resemble the elaborate word play in *Finnegans Wake* and in the novels of Raymond Roussel, but to insist on this resemblance would be to miss the point of the book. Louis Wolfson stands outside literature as we know it, and to do him justice we must read him on his own terms. For it is only in this way that we will be able to discover his book for what it is: one of those rare works that can change our perception of the world.

1974

Black on White
Recent paintings by David Reed

The hand of the painter has rarely instructed us in the ways of the hand. When we look at a painting, we see an accumulation of gestures, the layering and shaping of materials, the longing of the inanimate to take on life. But we do not see the hand itself. Like the God of the deists, it seems to have withdrawn from its own creation, or vanished into the density of the world it has made. It does not matter whether the painting is figurative or abstract: we confront the work as an object, and, as such, the surface remains independent of the will behind it.

In David Reed's new paintings, this has been reversed. Suddenly, the hand has been made visible to us, and in each horizontal stroke applied to the canvas, we are able to see that hand with such precision that it actually seems to be *moving*. Faithful only to itself, to the demands of the movement it brings forth, the hand is no longer a means to an end, but the substance of the object it creates. For each stroke we are given here is unique: there is no backtracking, no modeling, no pause. The hand moves across the surface in a single, unbroken gesture, and once this gesture has been completed, it is inviolate. The finished work is not a representation of this process – it is the process itself, and it asks to be *read* rather than simply observed. Composed of a series of rung-like strokes that descend the length of the canvas, each of these paintings resembles a vast poem without words. Our eyes follow its movement in the same way we follow a poem down a page, and just as the line in a poem is a unit of breath, so the line in the painting is a unit of gesture. For the language of these works is the language of the body.

Some people will probably try to see them as examples of minimal art. But that would be a mistake. Minimal art is an art of control, aiming at the rigorous ordering of visual information, while Reed's paintings are conceived in a way that sabotages the idea of a preordained result. It is this high degree of spontaneity within a consciously limited framework that produces such a harmonious coupling of intellectual and physical energies in his work. No two paintings are or can be exactly alike, even though each painting begins at the same point, with the same fundamental premises. For no matter how regular or controlled the gesture may be, its field of action is unstable, and in the end it is chance that governs the result. Because the white background is still wet when the horizontal strokes are applied, the painting can never be fully calculated in advance, and the image is always at the mercy of gravity. In some sense, then, each painting is born from a conflict between opposing forces. The horizontal stroke tries to impose an order upon the chaos of the background, and is deformed by it as the white paint settles. It would surely be stretching matters to interpret this as a parable of man against nature. And yet, because these paintings evolve in time, and because our reading of them necessarily leads us back through their whole history, we are able to re-enact this conflict whenever we come into their presence. What remains is the drama: and we begin to understand that, fundamentally, these works are the statement of that drama.

In the last sentence of Maurice Blanchot's novel, *Death Sentence*, the nameless narrator writes: 'And even more, let him try to imagine the hand that has written these pages: and if he is able to see it, then perhaps reading will become a serious task for him.' David Reed's new work is an expression of this same desire in the realm of painting. By allowing us to imagine his hand, by allowing us to *see* his hand, he has exposed us to the serious task of seeing: how we see and what we see, and how what we see in a painting is different from what we see anywhere else. It has taken considerable courage to do this. For it pushes the artist out from the shadows, leaving him with nowhere to stand but in the painting itself. And in order for us to look at one of these works, we have no choice but to go in there with him.

1975

Dada Bones

Of all the movements of the early avant-garde, Dada is the one that continues to say the most to us. Although its life was short – beginning in 1916 with the nightly spectacles at the Cabaret Voltaire in Zurich, and ending effectively, if not officially, in 1922 with the riotous demonstrations in Paris against Tristan Tzara's play, *Le Coeur à gaz* – its spirit has not quite passed into the remoteness of history. Even now, more than fifty years later, not a season goes by without some new book or exhibition about Dada, and it is with more than academic interest that we continue to investigate the questions it raised. For Dada's questions remain our questions, and when we speak of the relationship between art and society, of art versus action and art *as* action, we cannot help but turn to Dada as a source and as an example. We want to know about it not only for itself, but because we feel that it will help us toward an understanding of our own, present moment.

The diaries of Hugo Ball are a good place to begin. Ball, a key figure in the founding of Dada, was also the first defector from the Dada movement, and his record of the years between 1914 and 1921 is an extremely valuable document.* *Flight Out of Time* was originally published in Germany in 1927, shortly before Ball's death from stomach cancer at the age of forty-one, and it consists of passages that Ball extracted from his journals and edited with clear and partisan hindsight. It is not so much a self-portrait as an account of his inner progress, a spiritual and intellectual reckoning, and it moves from entry to entry in a rigorously dialectical manner. Although there are

---

**Flight Out of Time: A Dada Diary*, edited by John Elderfield and translated by Ann Raimes (Viking Press, 1975).

few biographical details, the sheer adventure of the thought is enough to hold us. For Ball was an incisive thinker; as a participant in early Dada, he is perhaps our finest witness to the Zurich group, and because Dada marked only one stage in his complex development, our view of it through his eyes gives us a kind of perspective we have not had before.

Hugo Ball was a man of his time, and to an extraordinary degree his life seems to embody the passions and contradictions of European society during the first quarter of this century. Student of Nietzsche's work; stage manager and playwright for the Expressionist theatre; left-wing journalist; vaudeville pianist; poet; novelist; author of works on Bakunin, the German Intelligentsia, early Christianity, and the writings of Hermann Hesse; convert to Catholicism: he seemed, at one moment or another, to have touched on nearly all the political and artistic preoccupations of the age. And yet, despite his many activities, Ball's attitudes and interests were remarkably consistent throughout his life, and in the end his entire career can be seen as a concerted, even feverish attempt to ground his existence in a fundamental truth, in a single, absolute reality. Too much an artist to be a philosopher, too much a philosopher to be an artist, too concerned with the fate of the world to think only in terms of personal salvation, and yet too inward to be an effective activist, Ball struggled toward solutions that could somehow answer both his inner and outer needs, and even in the deepest solitude he never saw himself as separate from the society around him. He was a man for whom everything came with great difficulty, whose sense of himself was never fixed, and whose moral integrity made him capable of brashly idealistic gestures totally out of keeping with his delicate nature. We have only to examine the famous photograph of Ball reciting a sound poem at the Cabaret Voltaire to understand this. He is dressed in an absurd costume that makes him look like a cross between the Tin Man and a demented bishop, and he stares out from under a high witch doctor's hat with an expression on his face of overwhelming terror. It is an unforgettable expression, and in this one image of him we have what amounts to a parable of his character, a perfect rendering of inside confronting outside, of darkness meeting darkness.

In the Prologue to *Flight Out of Time* Ball presents the reader with a cultural autopsy that sets the tone for all that follows: 'The world and society in 1913 looked like this: life is completely confined and shackled . . . The most burning question day and night is this: is there anywhere a force that is strong enough and above all vital enough to put an end to this state of affairs?' Elsewhere, in his 1917 lecture on Kandinsky, he states these ideas with even greater urgency: 'A thousand-year-old culture disintegrates. There are no columns and no supports, no foundations anymore – they have all been blown up . . . The meaning of the world has disappeared.' These feelings are not new to us. They confirm our sense of the European intellectual climate around the time of the First World War, and echo much of what we now take for granted as having formed the modern sensibility. What *is* unexpected, however, is what Ball says a little further on in the Prologue: 'It might seem as if philosophy had been taken over by the artists; as if the new impulses were coming from them; as if they were the prophets of rebirth. When we said Kandinsky and Picasso, we meant not painters, but priests; not craftsmen, but creators of new worlds and new paradises.' Dreams of total regeneration could exist side by side with the blackest pessimism, and for Ball there was no contradiction in this: both attitudes were part of a single approach. Art was not a way of turning from the problems of the world, it was a way of directly solving these problems. During his most difficult years, it was this faith that sustained Ball, from his early work in the theater – 'Only the theater is capable of creating the new society' – to his Kandinsky-influenced formulation of 'the union of all artistic mediums and forces', and beyond, to his Dada activities in Zurich.

The seriousness of these considerations, as elaborated in the diaries, helps to dispel several myths about the beginnings of Dada, above all the idea of Dada as little more than the sophomoric rantings of a group of young draft-dodgers, a kind of willful Marx Brothers zaniness. There was, of course, much that was plainly silly in the Cabaret performances, but for Ball this buffoonery was a means to an end, a necessary catharsis: 'Perfect scepticism makes perfect freedom possible . . . One can almost say that when belief in an object or a cause comes to an end, this object or cause returns to chaos and becomes common property. But perhaps it is necessary to have resolutely, forcibly produced chaos and thus a complete withdrawal of faith before an entirely new edifice can be built up on a changed basis of belief.' To understand Dada, then, at least in this early phase, we must see it as a vestige of old humanistic ideals, a reassertion of individual dignity in a mechanical age of standardization, as a *simultaneous* expression of despair and hope. Ball's particular contribution to the Cabaret performances, his sound poems, or 'poems without words', bears this out. Although he cast aside ordinary language, he had no intention of destroying language itself. In his almost mystical desire to recover what he felt to be a prelapsarian speech, Ball saw in this new, purely emotive form of poetry a way of capturing the magical essences of words. 'In these phonetic poems we totally renounce the language that journalism has abused and corrupted. We must return to the innermost alchemy of the word . . .'

Ball retreated from Zurich only seven months after the opening of the Cabaret Voltaire, partly from exhaustion, and partly from disenchantment with the way Dada was developing. His conflict was principally with Tzara, whose ambition was to turn Dada into one of the many movements of the international avant-garde. As John Elderfield summarizes in his introduction to Ball's diary: 'And once away he felt he discerned a certain "Dada hubris" in what they had been doing. He had believed they were eschewing conventional morality to elevate themselves as new men, that they had welcomed irrationalism as a way toward the "supernatural", that sensationalism was the best method of destroying the academic. He came to doubt all this – he had become ashamed of the confusion and eclecticism of the cabaret – and saw isolation from the age as a surer and more honest path toward these personal goals . . .' Several months later, however, Ball returned to Zurich to take part in the events of the Galerie Dada and to deliver his important lecture on Kandinsky, but within a short while he was again feuding with Tzara, and this time the break was final.

In July 1917, under Tzara's direction, Dada was officially launched as a movement, complete with its own publication, manifestos, and promotion campaign. Tzara was a tireless organizer, a true avant-gardist in the style of Marinetti, and eventually, with the help of Picabia and Serner, he led Dada far from the original ideas of the Cabaret Voltaire, away from what Elderfield correctly calls 'the earlier equilibrium of construction-negation' into the bravura of anti-art. A few years later there was a further split in the movement, and Dada divided itself into two factions: the German group, led by Huelsenbeck, George Grosz, and the Herzefelde brothers, which was predominantly political in approach, and Tzara's group, which moved to Paris in 1920, and which championed the aesthetic anarchism that ultimately developed into Surrealism.

If Tzara gave Dada its identity, he also robbed it of the moral purpose it had aspired to under Ball. By turning it into a doctrine, by garnishing it with a set of programmatic ideals, Tzara led Dada into self-contradiction and impotence. What for Ball had been a true cry from the heart against all systems of thought and action became one organization among others. The stance of anti-art, which opened the way for endless provocations and attacks, was essentially an inauthentic idea. For art opposed to art is nevertheless art; you can't have it both ways at once. As Tzara wrote in one of his manifestos: 'The true Dadaists are against Dada.' The impossibility of establishing this as dogma is obvious, and Ball, who had the foresight to realize this contradiction quite early, left as soon as he saw signs of Dada becoming a movement. For the others, however, Dada became a kind of bluff that was pushed to further and further extremes. But the real motivation was gone, and when Dada finally died, it was not so much from the battle it had fought as from its own inertia.

Ball's position, on the other hand, seems no less valid today than it did in 1917. Of what we have come to realize were several different periods and divergent tendencies in Dada, the moment of Ball's participation, as I see it, remains the moment of Dada's greatest strength, the period that speaks most persuasively to us today. This is perhaps a heretical view. But when we consider how Dada exhausted itself under Tzara, how it succumbed to the decadent system of exchange in the bourgeois art world, provoking the very audience whose favor it was courting, this branch of Dada must be seen as a symptom of art's essential weakness under modern capitalism – locked in the invisible cage of what Marcuse has called 'repressive tolerance'. But because Ball never treated Dada as an end in itself, he remained flexible, and was able to use Dada as an instrument for reaching higher goals, for producing a genuine critique of the age. Dada, for Ball, was merely the name for a kind of radical doubt, a way of sweeping aside all existing ideologies and moving on to an examination of the world around him. As such, the energy of Dada can never be used up: it is an idea whose time is always the present.

Ball's eventual return to the Catholicism of his childhood in 1921 is not really as strange as it may seem. It represents no true shift in his thinking, and in many ways can be seen as simply a further step in his development. Had he lived longer, there is no reason to believe that he would not have undergone further metamorphosis. As it is, we discover in his diaries a continual overlapping of ideas and concerns, so that even during the Dada period, for example, there are repeated references to Christianity ('I do not know if we will go beyond Wilde and Baudelaire in spite of all our efforts; or if we will not just remain romantics. There are probably other ways of achieving the miracle and other ways of opposition too – asceticism, for example, the church.') and during the time of his most serious Catholicism there is a preoccupation with mystical language that clearly resembles the sound poem theories of his Dada period. As he remarks in one of his last entries, in 1921: 'The socialist, the aesthete, the monk: all three agree that modern bourgeois education must be destroyed. The new ideal will take its new elements from all three.' Ball's short life was a constant straining toward a synthesis of these different points of view. If we regard him today as an important figure, it is not because he managed to discover a solution, but because he was able to state the problems with such clarity. In his intellectual courage, in the fervor of his confrontation with the world, Hugo Ball stands out as one of the exemplary spirits of the age.

1975

Truth, Beauty, Silence

Laura Riding was still in her thirties when she published her 477-page *Collected Poems* in 1938. At an age when most poets are just beginning to come into their own, she had already reached full maturity, and the list of her accomplishments in literature up to that time is impressive: nine volumes of poetry, several collections of critical essays and fiction, a long novel, and the founding of a small publishing house, the Seizin Press. As early as 1924, soon after her graduation from Cornell, *The Fugitive* had called her 'the discovery of the year, a new figure in American poetry', and later, in Europe, during the period of her intimate and stormy relationship with Robert Graves, she became an important force of the international avant-garde. Young Auden was apparently so influenced by her poems that Graves felt obliged to write him a letter reprimanding him for his blatant Laura Riding imitations, and the method of close textual criticism developed in *A Survey of Modernist Poetry* (written in collaboration with Graves) directly inspired Empson's *Seven Types of Ambiguity*. Then, after 1938, nothing. No more poems, no more stories, no more essays. As time went on, Laura Riding's name was almost totally forgotten, and to a new generation of poets and writers it was as if she had never existed.

She was not heard from again until 1962, when she agreed to give a reading of some of her poems for a BBC broadcast and to deliver a few remarks about the philosophical and linguistic reasons for her break with poetry. Since then, there have been several appearances in print, and now, most recently, the publication of two books: a selection of her poems, which is prefaced by a further discussion of her attitude toward poetry, and *The Telling*, a prose work which she has described as a 'personal evangel'. Clearly, Laura Riding is back. Although she has written no poems since 1938, her new work in *The Telling* is intimately connected with her earlier writings, and in spite of her long public silence, her career is of a single piece. Laura Riding and Laura (Riding) Jackson – the married name she now uses – are in many ways mirror images of one another. Each has attempted to realize a kind of universal truth in language, a way of speaking that would somehow reveal to us our essential humanness – 'a linguistically ordained ideal, every degree of fulfillment of which is a degree of express fulfillment of the hope comprehended in being, in its comprehending us within it, as human' – and if this ambition seems at times to be rather grandiosely stated, it has nevertheless been constant. The only thing that has changed is the method. Up to 1938, Laura Riding was convinced that poetry was the best way to achieve this goal. Since then, she has revised her opinion, and has not only given up poetry, but now sees it as one of the prime obstacles on this path toward linguistic truth.

When we turn to her own poetry, what is above all striking is its consistency of purpose and manner. From the very beginning, it seems, Laura Riding knew where she was going, and her poems ask to be read not as isolated lyrics, but as interconnecting parts of an enormous poetic project.

> We must learn better
> What we are and are not.
> We are not the wind.
> We are not every vagrant mood that tempts
> Our minds to giddy homelessness.
> We must distinguish better
> Between ourselves and strangers.
> There is much that we are not.
> There is much that is not.
> There is much that we have not to be.
> (*from* 'The Why of the Wind')

This is essential Riding: the abstract level of discourse, the insistence upon confronting ultimate questions, the tendency toward moral exhortation, the quickness and cleanness of thought, the unexpected juxtapositions of words, as in the phrase 'giddy homelessness'. The physical world is hardly present here, and when it is mentioned, it appears only as metaphor, as a kind of linguistic shorthand for indicating ideas and mental processes. The wind, for example, is not a real wind, but a way of expressing what is changeable, a reference to the idea of flux, and we feel its impact only as an idea. The poem itself proceeds as an argument rather than as a statement of feeling or an evocation of personal experience, and its movement is toward generalization, toward the utterance of what the poet takes to be a fundamental truth.

'We are not the wind.' In other words, we are what does not change. For Laura Riding, this is the given of her project; it cannot be proved, but nevertheless operates as the informing principle of her work as a whole. In poem after poem we witness her trying somehow to peel back the skin of the world in order to find some absolute and unassailable place of permanence, and because the poems are rarely grounded in a physical perception of that world, they tend, strangely, to exist in an almost purely emotional climate, created by the fervor of this metaphysical quest. And yet, in spite of the high seriousness of the poems, there are moments of sharp wit that remind us of Emily Dickinson:

> Then follows a description
> Of an interval called death
> By the living.
> But I shall speak of it
> As of a brief illness.
> For it lasted only
> From being not ill
> To being not ill.

> It came about by chance –
> I met God.
> 'What,' he said, 'you already?'
> 'What,' I said, 'you still?'
> (*from* 'Then Follows', in *Collected Poems*)

In the beginning, it is difficult to take the full measure of these poems, to understand the particular kinds of problems they are trying to deal with. Laura Riding gives us almost nothing to see, and this absence of imagery and sensuous detail, of any true *surface*, is at first baffling. We feel as though we had been blinded. But this is intentional on her part, and it plays an important role in the themes she develops. She does not so much want us to see as to consider the notion of what is seeable.

> You have pretended to be seeing.
> I have pretended that you saw.
> So came we by such eyes –
> And within mystery to have language.
>
> *
>
> There was no sight to see.
> That which is to be seen is no sight.
> You made it a sight to see.
> It is no sight, and this was the cause.
>
> Now, having seen, let our eyes close
> And a dark blessing pass among us –
> A quick-slow blessing to have seen
> And said and done no worse or better.
> (*from* 'Benedictory')

The only thing that seems to be present here is the poet's voice, and it is only gradually, as we 'let our eyes close', that we begin to listen to this voice with special care, to become extremely sensitive to its nuances. Malebranche said that attention is the natural prayer of the soul. In her best poems, I think, Laura Riding coaxes us into a state of rapt listening, *into* a voice to which we give our complete attention, so that we, as readers, become participants in the unfolding of the poem. The voice is not so much speaking out loud as thinking, following the complex process of thought, and in such a way that it is almost immediately internalized by us. Few poets have ever been able to manipulate abstractions so persuasively. Having been stripped of ornament, reduced to their bare essentials, the poems emerge as a kind of rhetoric, a system of pure argument that works in the manner of music, generating an interaction of themes and counter-themes, and giving the same formal pleasures that music gives.

> And talk in talk like time in time vanishes.
> Ringing changes on dumb supposition,
> Conversation succeeds conversation,
> Until there's nothing left to talk about
> Except truth, the perennial monologue,
> And no talker to dispute it but itself.
>   (*from* 'The Talking World')

These strengths, however, can also be weaknesses. For in order to sustain the high degree of intellectual precision necessary to the success of the poems, Laura Riding has been forced to engage in a kind of poetic brinkmanship, and she has often lost more than she has won. Eventually, we come to realize that the reasons for her break with poetry are implicit in the poems themselves. No matter how much we might admire her work, we sense that there is something missing in it, that it is not really capable of expressing the full range of experience it claims to be expressing. The source of this lack, paradoxically, lies in her conception of language, which in many ways is at odds with the very idea of poetry:

> Come, words, away from mouths,
> Away from tongues in mouths

> And reckless hearts in tongues
> And mouths in cautious heads –
>
> Come, words, away to where
> The meaning is not thickened
> With the voice's fretting substance . . .
>> (*from* 'Come, Words, Away')

This is a self-defeating desire. If anything, poetry is precisely that way of using language which forces words to remain *in* the mouth, the way by which we can most fully experience and understand 'the voice's fretting substance'. There is something too glacial in Laura Riding's approach to gain our sympathy. If the truth in language she is seeking is a human truth, it would seem to be contradictory to want this truth at the expense of what is human. But in trying to deny speech its physical properties – in refusing to acknowledge that speech is an imperfect tool of imperfect creatures – this seems to be exactly what she is doing.

In the 1938 preface to the *Collected Poems*, at the moment of her most passionate adherence to poetry, we can see this desire for transcendence as the motivating force behind her work. 'I am going to give you', she writes, 'poems written for all the reasons of poetry – poems which are also a record of how, by gradual integration of the reasons of poetry, existence in poetry becomes more real than existence in time – more real because more good, more good because more true.' Thirty years later, she uses almost the same terms to justify her equally passionate opposition to poetry: 'To a poet the mere making of a poem can seem to solve the problem of truth . . . But only a problem of art is solved in poetry. Art, whose honesty must work through artifice, cannot avoid cheating truth. Poetic art cheats truth to further and finer degrees than art of any other kind because the spoken word is its exclusive medium . . .'

For all their loftiness and intensity, these statements remain curiously vague. For the truth that is referred to is never really defined, except as something beyond time, beyond art, beyond the senses. Such talk seems to set us afloat in a vast realm of Platonic idealism, and it is difficult for us to know where we are. At the same time, we are unconvinced. Neither statement is very believable to us as a statement about poetry, because, at heart, neither one *is* about poetry. Laura Riding is clearly interested in problems that extend beyond the scope of poetry, and by dwelling on these problems *as if* they were poetry's exclusive concerns, she only confuses the issue. She did not renounce poetry because of any objective inadequacy in poetry itself – for it is no more or less adequate than any other human activity – but because poetry as she conceived of it was no longer capable of saying what she wanted to say. She now feels that she had 'reached poetry's limit'. But what really happened, it would seem, is that she had reached her own limit in poetry.

It is appropriate, then, that her work since 1938 has been largely devoted to a more general investigation of language, and when we come to *The Telling* we find a deeper discussion of many of the same questions she had tried to formulate in her poetry. The book, which fits into no established literary category, is positively Talmudic in structure. 'The Telling' itself is a short text of less than fifty pages, divided into numbered paragraphs, originally written for an issue of the magazine, *Chelsea*, in 1967. To this 'core-text', which is written in a dense, highly abstract prose almost totally devoid of outside references, she has added a series of commentaries, commentaries on commentaries, notes, and addenda, which flesh out many of the earlier conclusions and treat of various literary, political, and philosophical matters. It is an astonishing display of a consciousness confronting and examining itself. Based on the idea that 'the human utmost is marked out in a linguistic utmost', she pursues an ideal of 'humanly perfect word-use' (as opposed to 'artistically perfect word-use'), by which she aims to uncover the essential nature of being. Again, or rather still, she is straining toward absolutes, toward an unshakable and unified vision of the world:

'. . . the nature of our being is not to be known as we know the weather, which is by the sense of the momentary. Weather is all change, while our being, in its human nature, is all constancy . . . it is to be known only by the sense of the constant.' Although Laura (Riding) Jackson has put her former poet self in parentheses, she looks upon *The Telling* as the successful continuation of her efforts as a poet: 'To speak as I speak in it, say such things as I say in it, was part of my hope as a poet.'

The first paragraph of 'The Telling' sets forth the substance of the problem that she confronts in the rest of the book:

> There is something to be told about us for the telling of which we all wait. In our unwilling ignorance we hurry to listen to stories of old human life, new human life, fancied human life, avid of something to while away the time of unanswered curiosity. We know we are explainable, and not explained. Many of the lesser things concerning us have been told, but the greater things have not been told; and nothing can fill their place. Whatever we learn of what is not ourselves, but ours to know, being of our universal world, will likewise leave the emptiness an emptiness. Until the missing story of ourselves is told, nothing besides told can suffice us: we shall go on quietly craving it.

What immediately strikes us here is the brilliance of the writing itself. The quiet urgency and strong, cadenced phrasing entice us to go on listening. It seems that we are about to be told something radically different from anything we have ever been told before, and of such fundamental importance that it would be in our best interests to pay careful attention to what follows. 'We know we are explainable, and not explained.' In the subsequent paragraphs we are shown why the various human disciplines – science, religion, philosophy, history, poetry – have not and cannot explain us. Suddenly, everything has been swept aside; the way seems to have been cleared for a totally fresh approach to things. And yet, when she reaches the point of offering her own explanations, we are once again presented with the mysterious and unbelievable Platonism we had encountered before. It seems, finally, as if she were rejecting the myth-making tendencies of previous thought only in order to present another myth of her own devising – a myth of memory, a faith in the capacity of human beings to remember a time of wholeness that preceded the existence of individual selves. 'May our Mayness become All-embracing. May we see in one another the All that was once All-One re-become One.' And elsewhere: 'Yes, I think we remember our creation! – have the memory of it in us, to know. Through the memory of it we apprehend that there was a Before-time of being from which being passed into what would be us.' The problem is not that we doubt this belief of hers. We feel, in fact, that she is trying to report back to us about a genuine mystical experience; what is hard for us to accept is that she assumes this experience to be accessible to everyone. Perhaps it is. But we have no way of knowing – and would have no way of proving it even if we did. Laura (Riding) Jackson speaks of this purely personal experience in rigorous and objective terms, and as a result mingles two kinds of incompatible discourse. Her private perceptions have been projected on to the world at large, so that when she looks out on that world she thinks she sees a confirmation of her findings. But there is no distinction made between what is asserted as fact and what is verifiable as fact. As a consequence, there is no common ground established with us, and we find no place where we would want to stand with her in her beliefs.

In spite of this, however, it would be wrong simply to dismiss the book. If *The Telling* ultimately fails to carry out its promises, it is still valuable to us for the exceptional quality of its prose and the innovations of its form. The sheer immensity of its ambitions makes it an exciting work, even when it is most irritating. More importantly, it is crucial to us for what it reveals – retroactively – about Laura Riding's earlier work as a poet. For, in the end, it is as a poet that she will be read and remembered. Whatever objections we might want to raise about her approach to poetry in general, it would be difficult not to recognize her as a poet of importance. We need not be in agreement with her to admire her.

> Roses are buds, and beautiful,
> One petal leaning toward adventure.
> Roses are full, all petals forward,
> Beauty and power indistinguishable.
> Roses are blown, startled with life,
> Death young in their faces.
> Then comes the halt, and recumbence, and failing.
> But none says, 'A rose is dead.'
> But men die: it is said, it is seen.
> For man is a long, late adventure;
> His budding is a purpose,
> His fullness more purpose,
> His blowing a renewal,
> His death a cramped spilling
> Of rash measures and miles.
> To the rose no tears:
> Which flee before the race is called.
> And to the man no mercy but his will:
> That he had had his will, and is done.
> The mercy of truth – it is to be truth.
> *(from* 'The Last Covenant')

In one of the supplementary chapters of *The Telling*, 'Extracts From Communications', she speaks of the relationship between the writer and his work in a way that seems to express her aspirations as a poet. 'If what you write is true, it will not be so because of what you are as a writer but because of what you are as a being. There can be no literary equivalent to truth. If, in writing, truth is the quality of what is said, told, this is not a literary achievement: it is a simple human achievement.' This is not very far from the spirit of Ben Jonson's assertion that only a good man is capable of writing a good poem. It is an idea that stands at one extreme of our literary consciousness, and it places poetry within an essentially moral framework. As a poet, Laura Riding followed this principle until she reached what she felt to be 'a crisis-point at which division between craft and creed reveals itself to be absolute'. In the making of poems, she concluded, the demands of art would always outweigh the demands of truth.

Beauty and truth. It is the old question, come back to haunt us. Laura Riding sacrificed her poetic career in a choice between the two. But whether she has really answered the question, as she appears to think she has, is open to debate. What we do have are the poems she left behind her, and it is not surprising, perhaps, that we are drawn to them most of all for their beauty. We cannot call Laura Riding a neglected poet, since she was the cause of her own neglect. But after more than thirty years of absence, these poems strike us with all the force of a rediscovery.

1975

From Cakes to Stones
A note on Beckett's French

Mercier and Camier was the first of Samuel Beckett's novels to be written in French. Completed in 1946, and withheld from publication until 1970, it is also the last of his longer works to have been translated into English. Such a long delay would seem to indicate that Beckett is not overly fond of the work. Had he not been given the Nobel prize in 1969, in fact, it seems likely that *Mercier and Camier* would not have been published at all. This reticence on Beckett's part is somewhat puzzling. For if *Mercier and Camier* is clearly a transitional work, at once harking back to *Murphy* and *Watt* and looking forward to the masterpieces of the early fifties, it is nevertheless a brilliant work, with its own particular strengths and charms, unduplicated in any of Beckett's six other novels. Even at his not quite best, Beckett remains Beckett, and reading him is like reading no one else.

Mercier and Camier are two men of indeterminate middle age who decide to leave everything behind them and set off on a journey. Like Flaubert's Bouvard and Pécuchet, like Laurel and Hardy, like the other 'pseudo couples' in Beckett's work, they are not so much separate characters as two elements of a tandem reality, and neither one could exist without the other. The purpose of their journey is never stated, nor is their destination ever made clear. 'They had consulted together at length, before embarking on this journey, weighing with all the calm at their command what benefits they might hope from it, what ills apprehend, maintaining turn about the dark side and the rosy. The only certitude they gained from these debates was that of not lightly launching out, into the unknown.' Beckett, the master of the comma, manages in these few sentences to cancel out any possibility of a goal. Quite simply, Mercier and Camier agree to meet, they meet (after painful confusion), and set off. That they never really get anywhere, only twice, in fact, cross the town limits, in no way impedes the progress of the book. For the book is not about what Mercier and Camier do; it is about what they are.

Nothing happens. Or, more precisely, what happens is what does not happen. Armed with the vaudeville props of umbrella, sack, and raincoat, the two heroes meander through the town and the surrounding countryside, encountering various objects and personages: they pause frequently and at length in an assortment of bars and public places; they consort with a warm-hearted prostitute named Helen; they kill a policeman; they gradually lose their few possessions and drift apart. These are the outward events, all precisely told, with wit, elegance, and pathos, and interspersed with some beautiful descriptive passages ('The sea is not far, just visible beyond the valleys disappearing eastward, pale plinth as pale as the pale wall of sky'). But the real substance of the book lies in the conversations between Mercier and Camier:

> If we have nothing to say, said Camier, let us say nothing.
> We have things to say, said Mercier.
> Then why can't we say them? said Camier.
> We can't, said Mercier.
> Then let us be silent, said Camier.
> But we try, said Mercier.

In a celebrated passage of *Talking about Dante*, Mandelstam wrote: 'The *Inferno* and especially the *Purgatorio* glorify the human gait, the measure and rhythm of walking, the foot and its shape . . . In Dante philosophy and poetry are forever on the move, forever on their feet. Even standing still is a variety of accumulated motion; making a place for people to stand and talk takes as much trouble as scaling an Alp.' Beckett, who is one of the finest readers of Dante, has learned these lessons with utter thoroughness. Almost uncannily, the prose of *Mercier and Camier* moves along at a walking pace, and after a while one begins to have the distinct impression that somewhere, buried deep within the words, a silent metronome is beating out the rhythms of Mercier and Camier's perambulations. The pauses, the hiatuses, the sudden shifts of conversation and description do not break this rhythm, but rather take place under its influence (which has already been firmly established), so that their effect is not one of disruption but of counterpoint and fulfillment. A mysterious stillness seems to envelop each sentence in the book, a kind of gravity, or calm, so that between each sentence the reader feels the passing of time, the footsteps that continue to move, even when nothing is said. 'Sitting at the bar they discoursed of this and that, brokenly, as was their custom. They spoke, fell silent, listened to each other, stopped listening, each as he fancied or as bidden from within.'

This notion of time, of course, is directly related to the notion of *timing*, and it seems no accident that *Mercier and Camier* immediately precedes *Waiting for Godot* in Beckett's *oeuvre*. In some sense, it can be seen as a warm-up for the play. The music-hall banter, which was perfected in the dramatic works, is already present in the novel:

> What will it be? said the barman.
> When we need you we'll tell you, said Camier.
> What will it be? said the barman.
> The same as before, said Mercier.
> You haven't been served, said the barman.
> The same as this gentleman, said Mercier.
> The barman looked at Camier's empty glass.
> I forget what it was, he said.
> I too, said Camier.
> I never knew, said Mercier.

But whereas *Waiting for Godot* is sustained by the implicit drama of Godot's absence – an absence that commands the scene as powerfully as any presence – *Mercier and Camier* progresses in a void. From one moment to the next, it is impossible to foresee what will happen. The action, which is not buoyed by any tension or intrigue, seems to take place against a background of nearly total silence, and whatever is said is said at the very moment there is nothing left to say. Rain dominates the book, from the first paragraph to the last sentence ('And in the dark he could hear better too, he could hear the sounds the long day had kept from him, human murmurs for example, and the rain on the water.') – an endless Irish rain, which is accorded the status of a metaphysical idea, and which creates an atmosphere that hovers between boredom and anguish, between bitterness and jocularity. As in the play, tears are shed, but more from a knowledge of the futility of tears that from any need to purge oneself of grief. Likewise, laughter is merely what happens when tears have been spent. All goes on, slowly waning in the hush of time, and unlike Vladimir and Estragon, Mercier and Camier must endure without any hope of redemption.

The key word in all this, I feel, is dispossession. Beckett, who begins with little, ends with even less. The movement in each of his works is toward a kind of unburdening, by which he leads us to the limits of experience – to a place where aesthetic and moral judgments become inseparable. This is the itinerary of the characters in his books, and it has also been his own progress as a writer. From the lush, convoluted, and jaunty prose of *More Pricks than Kicks* (1934) to the desolate spareness of *The Lost Ones* (1970), he has gradually cut closer and closer to the bone. His decision thirty years ago to write in French was undoubtedly the crucial event in this progress. This was an almost inconceivable act. But again, Beckett is not like other writers. Before truly coming into his own, he had to leave behind what came most easily to him, struggle *against* his own facility as a stylist. Beyond Dickens and Joyce, there is perhaps no English writer of the past hundred years who has equalled Beckett's early prose for vigor and intelligence; the language of *Murphy*, for example, is so packed that the novel has the density of a short lyric poem. By switching to French (a language, as Beckett has remarked, that 'has no style'), he willingly began all over again. *Mercier and Camier* stands at the very beginning of this new life, and it is interesting to note that in this English translation Beckett has cut out nearly a fifth of the original text. Phrases, sentences, entire passages have been discarded, and what we have been given is really an editing job as well as a translation. This tampering, however, is not difficult to understand. Too many echoes, too many ornate and clever flourishes from the past remain, and though a considerable amount of superb material has been lost, Beckett apparently did not think it good enough to keep.

In spite of this, or perhaps because of this, *Mercier and Camier* comes close to being a flawless work. As with all of Beckett's self-translations, this version is not so much a literal translation of the original as a re-creation, a 'repatriation' of the book into English. However stripped his style in French may be, there is always a little extra something added to the English renderings, some slight twist of diction or nuance, some unexpected word falling at just the right moment, that reminds us that English is nevertheless Beckett's home.

> George, said Camier, five sandwiches, four wrapped and one on the side. You see, he said, turning graciously to Mr Conaire, I think of everything. For the one I eat here will give me the strength to get back with the four others.
>
> Sophistry, said Mr Conaire. You set off with your five, wrapped, feel faint, open up, take one out, eat, recuperate, push on with the others.
>
> For all response Camier began to eat.
>
> You'll spoil him, said Mr Conaire. Yesterday cakes, today sandwiches, tomorrow crusts, and Thursday stones.
>
> Mustard, said Camier.

There is a crispness to this that outdoes the French. 'Sophistry' for 'raisonnement du clerc', 'crusts' for 'pain sec', and the assonance with 'mustard' in the next sentence give a neatness and economy to the exchange that is even more satisfying than the original. Everything has been pared down to a minimum; not a syllable is out of place.

We move from cakes to stones, and from page to page Beckett builds a world out of almost nothing. Mercier and Camier set out on a journey and do not go anywhere. But at each step of the way, we want to be exactly where they are. How Beckett manages this is something of a mystery. But as in all his work, less is more.

1975

The Poetry of Exile

A Jew, born in Romania, who wrote in German and lived in France. Victim of the Second World War, survivor of the death camps, suicide before he was fifty. Paul Celan was a poet of exile, an outsider even to the language of his own poems, and if his life was exemplary in its pain, a paradigm of the destruction and dislocation of mid-century Europe, his poetry is defiantly idiosyncratic, always and absolutely his own. In Germany, he is considered the equal of Rilke and Trakl, the heir to Hölderlin's metaphysical lyricism, and elsewhere his work is held in similar esteem, prompting statements such as George Steiner's recent remark that Celan is 'almost certainly the major European poet of the period after 1945'. At the same time, Celan is an exceedingly difficult poet, both dense and obscure. He demands so much of a reader, and in his later work his utterances are so gnomic, that it is nearly impossible to make full sense of him, even after many readings. Fiercely intelligent, propelled by a dizzying linguistic force, Celan's poems seem to explode on the page, and encountering them for the first time is a memorable event. It is to feel the same strangeness and excitement that one feels in discovering the work of Hopkins, or Emily Dickinson.

Czernovitz, Bukovina, where Celan was born as Paul Anczel in 1920, was a multilingual area that had once been part of the Habsburg Empire. In 1940, after the Hitler-Stalin pact, it was annexed by the Soviet Union, in the following year occupied by Nazi troops, and in 1943 retaken by the Russians. Celan's parents were deported to a concentration camp in 1942 and did not return; Celan, who managed to escape, was put in a labor camp until December 1943. In 1945 he went to Bucharest, where he worked as a translator and publisher's reader, then moved to Vienna in 1947, and finally, in 1948, settled permanently in Paris, where he married and became a teacher of German literature at the Ecole Normale Supérieure. His output comprises seven books of poetry and translations of more than two dozen foreign poets, including Mandelstam, Ungaretti, Pessoa, Rimbaud, Valéry, Char, du Bouchet, and Dupin.

Celan came to poetry rather late, and his first poems were not published until he was almost thirty. All his work, therefore, was written after the Holocaust, and his poems are everywhere informed by its memory. The unspeakable yields a poetry that continually threatens to overwhelm the limits of what can be spoken. For Celan forgot nothing, forgave nothing. The death of his parents and his own experiences during the war are recurrent and obsessive themes that run through all his work.

> With names, watered
> by every exile.
> With names and seeds,
> with names dipped
> into all
> the calyxes that are full of your
> regal blood, man, – into all
> the calyxes of the great
> ghetto-rose, from which
> you look at us, immortal with so many
> deaths died on morning errands.
> (*from* 'Crowned Out . . .', 1963, trans. by Michael Hamburger)

Even after the war, Celan's life remained an unstable one. He suffered acutely from feelings of persecution, which led to repeated breakdowns in his later years – and eventually to his suicide in 1970, when he drowned himself in the Seine. An incessant writer who produced hundreds of poems during his relatively short writing life, Celan poured all his grief and anger into his work. There is no poetry more furious than his, no poetry so purely inspired by bitterness. Celan never stopped confronting the dragon of the past, and in the end it swallowed him up.

'Todesfugue' (Death Fugue) is not Celan's best poem, but it is unquestionably his most famous poem – the work that made his reputation. Coming as it did in the late forties, only a few years after the end of the war – and in striking contrast to Adorno's rather fatuous remark about the 'barbarity' of writing poems after Auschwitz – 'Todesfugue' had a considerable impact among German readers, both for its direct mention of the concentration camps and for the terrible beauty of its form. The poem is literally a fugue composed of words, and its pounding, rhythmical repetitions and variations mark off a terrain no less circumscribed, no less closed in on itself than a prison surrounded by barbed wire. Covering slightly less than two pages, it begins and ends with the following stanzas:

> Black milk of dawn we drink it at dusk
> we drink it at noon and at daybreak we drink it at night
> we drink and we drink
> we are digging a grave in the air there's room for us all
> A man lives in the house he plays with the serpents he writes
> he writes when it darkens to Germany your golden hair Margarete
> he writes it and steps outside and the stars all aglisten he whistles for his hounds
> he whistles for his Jews he has them dig a grave in the earth
> he commands us to play for the dance

> *

> Black milk of dawn we drink you at night
> we drink you at noon death is a master from Germany
> we drink you at dusk and at daybreak we drink and we drink you
> death is a master from Germany his eye is blue

> he shoots you with bullets of lead his aim is true
> a man lives in the house your golden hair Margarete
> he sets his hounds on us he gives us a grave in the air
> he plays with the serpents and dreams death is a master
>   from Germany
> your golden hair Margarete
> your ashen hair Shulamite
>
> (trans. by Joachim Neugroschel)

In spite of the poem's great control and the formal sublimation of an impossibly emotional theme, 'Todesfugue' is one of Celan's most explicit works. In the sixties, he even turned against it, refusing permission to have it reprinted in more anthologies because he felt that his poetry had progressed to a stage where 'Todesfugue' was too obvious and superficially realistic. With this in mind, however, one does discover in this poem elements common to much of Celan's work: the taut energy of the language, the objectification of private anguish, the unusual distancing effected between feeling and image. As Celan himself expressed it in an early commentary on his poems: 'What matters for this language . . . is precision. It does not transfigure, does not "poetize", it names and composes, it tries to measure out the sphere of the given and the possible.'

This notion of the possible is central to Celan. It is the way by which one can begin to enter his conception of the poem, his vision of reality. For the seeming paradox of another of his statements – 'Reality is not. It must be searched for and won' – can lead to confusion unless one has already understood the aspiration for the real that informs Celan's poetry. Celan is not advocating a retreat into subjectivity or the construction of an imaginary universe. Rather, he is staking out the distance over which the poem must travel and defining the ambiguity of a world in which all values have been subverted.

> Speak –
> But keep yes and no unsplit,

And give your say this meaning:
give it the shade.

Give it shade enough,
give it as much
as you know has been dealt out between
midday and midday and midnight.

Look around:
look how it all leaps alive –
where death is! Alive!
He speaks truly who speaks the shade.
(*from* 'Speak, You Also', trans. by Michael Hamburger)

In a public address delivered in the city of Bremen in 1958 after being awarded an important literary prize, Celan spoke of language as the one thing that had remained intact for him after the war, even though it had to pass through 'the thousand darknesses of death-bringing speech'. 'In this language,' Celan said – and by this he meant German, the language of the Nazis and the language of his poems – 'I have tried to write poetry, in order to acquire a perspective of reality for myself.' He then compared the poem to a message in a bottle – thrown out to sea in the hope that it will one day wash up to land, 'perhaps on the shore of the heart'. 'Poems', he continued, 'even in this sense are under way: they are heading toward something. Toward what? Toward some open place that can be inhabited, toward a thou which can be addressed, perhaps toward a reality which can be addressed.'

The poem, then, is not a transcription of an already known world, but a process of discovery, and the act of writing for Celan is one that demands personal risks. Celan did not write solely in order to express himself, but to orient himself within his own life and take his stand in the world, and it is this feeling of necessity that communicates itself to a reader. These poems are more than literary artifacts. They are a means of staying alive.

In a 1946 essay on Van Gogh, Meyer Schapiro refers to the notion of realism in a way that could also apply to Celan. 'I do not mean realism in the repugnant, narrow sense that it has acquired today,' Professor Schapiro writes, '. . . but rather the sentiment that external reality is an object of strong desire or need, as a possession and potential means of fulfillment of the striving human being, and is therefore the necessary ground of art.' Then, quoting a phrase from one of Van Gogh's letters – 'I'm terrified of getting away from the possible . . .' – he observes: 'Struggling against the perspective that diminishes an individual object before his eyes, he renders it larger than life. The loading of the pigment is in part a reflex of this attitude, a frantic effort to preserve in the image of things their tangible matter and to create something equally solid and concrete on the canvas.'

Celan, whose life and attitude toward his art closely parallel Van Gogh's, used language in a way that is not unlike the way Van Gogh used paints, and their work is surprisingly similar in spirit.* Neither Van Gogh's stroke nor Celan's syntax is strictly representational, for in the eyes of each the 'objective' world is interlocked with his perception of it. There is no reality that can be posited without the simultaneous effort to penetrate it, and the work of art as an ongoing process bears witness to this desire. Just as Van Gogh's painted objects acquire a concreteness 'as real as reality', Celan handles words as if they had the density of objects, and he endows them with a substantiality that enables them to become a part of the world, his world – and not simply its mirror.

Celan's poems resist straightforward exegesis. They are not linear progressions, moving from word to word, from point A

---

*Celan makes reference to Van Gogh in several of his poems, and the kinship between the poet and painter is indeed quite strong: both began as artists in their late twenties after having lived through experiences that marked them deeply for the rest of their lives; both produced work prolifically, at a furious pace, as if depending on the work for their very survival; both underwent debilitating mental crises that led to confinement; both committed suicide, foreigners in France.

to point B. Rather, they present themselves to a reader as intricate networks of semantic densities. Interlingual puns, oblique personal references, intentional misquotations, bizarre neologisms: these are the sinews that bind Celan's poems together. It is not possible to keep up with him, to follow his drift at every step along the way. One is guided more by a sense of tone and intention than by textual scrutiny. Celan does not speak explicitly, but he never fails to make himself clear. There is nothing random in his work, no gratuitous elements to obscure the perception of the poem. One reads with one's skin, as if by osmosis, unconsciously absorbing nuances, overtones, syntactical twists, which in themselves are as much the meaning of poem as its analytic content. Celan's method of composition is not unlike that of Joyce in *Finnegans Wake*. But if Joyce's art was one of accumulation and expansion – a spiral whirling into infinity – Celan's poetry is continually collapsing into itself, negating its very premises, again and again arriving at zero. We are in the world of the absurd, but we have been led there by a mind that refuses to acquiesce to it.

Consider the following poem, 'Largo', one of Celan's later poems – and a typical example of the difficulty a reader faces in tackling Celan.* In Michael Hamburger's translation it reads:

You of the same mind, moor-wandering near one:

more-than-
death-
sized we lie
together, autumn
crocuses, the timeless, teems
under our breathing eyelids,

---

*I am grateful to Katharine Washburn, a scrupulous reader and translator of Celan, for help in deciphering the German text of this poem and suggesting possible references.

the pair of blackbirds hangs
beside us, under
our whitely drifting
companions up there, our

meta-
stases.

The German text, however, reveals things that necessarily elude the grasp of translation:

Gleichsinnige du, heidegängerisch Nahe:

über-
sterbens-
gross liegen
wir beieinander, die Zeit-
lose wimmelt
dir unter den atmenden Lidern,

Das Amselpaar hängt
neben uns, unter
unsern gemeinsam droben mit-
ziehenden weissen

Meta-
stasen.

In the first line, *heidegängerisch* is an inescapable allusion to Heidegger – whose thinking was in many ways close to Celan's, but who, as a pro-Nazi, stood on the side of the murderers. Celan visited Heidegger in the sixties, and although it is not known what they said to each other, one can assume that they discussed Heidegger's position during the war. The reference to Heidegger in the poem is underscored by the use of some of the central words from his philosophical writings: *Nahe*, *Zeit*, etc. This is Celan's way: he does not mention anything directly, but weaves his meanings into the fabric of the language, creating a space for the invisible, in the same way that thought accompanies us as we move through a landscape.

Further along, in the third stanza, there are the two blackbirds (stock figures in fairy tales, who speak in riddles and bring bad tidings). In the German one reads *Amsel* – which echoes the sound of Celan's own name, Anczel. At the same time, there is an evocation of Günter Grass's novel, *Dog Years*, which chronicles the love–hate relationship between a Jew and a Nazi during the war. The Jewish character in the story is named Amsel, and throughout the book – to quote George Steiner again – 'there is a deadly pastiche of the metaphysical jargon of Heidegger'.

Toward the end of the poem, the presence of 'our whitely drifting / companions up there' is a reference to the Jewish victims of the Holocaust: the smoke of the bodies burned in crematoria. From early poems such as 'Todesfugue' ('he gives us a grave in the air') to later poems such as 'Largo', the Jewish dead in Celan's work inhabit the air, are the very substance we are condemned to breathe: souls turned into smoke, into dust, into nothing at all – 'our / meta- / stases'.

Celan's preoccupation with the Holocaust goes beyond mere history, however. It is the primal moment, the first cause and last effect of an entire cosmology. Celan is essentially a religious poet, and although he speaks with the voice of one forsaken by God, he never abandons the struggle to make sense of what has no sense, to come to grips with his own Jewishness. Negation, blasphemy, and irony take the place of devotion; the forms of righteousness are mimicked; Biblical phrases are turned around, subverted, made to speak against themselves. But in so doing, Celan draws ever nearer to the source of his despair, the absence that lives in the heart of all things. Much has been said about Celan's 'negative theology'. It is most fully expressed in the opening stanzas of 'Psalm':

No One kneads us anew from earth and clay,
no one addresses our dust.
No One.

Laudeamus te, No One.
For your sake would we
bloom forth:
unto
You.

Nothing
were we, and are we and
will be, all abloom:
this Nothing's-, this
no-man's-rose.
     (trans. by Katharine Washburn)

In the last decade of his life, Celan gradually refined his work to a point where he began to enter new and uncharted territory. The long lines and ample breath of the early poems give way to an elliptical, almost panting style in which words are broken up into their component syllables, unorthodox word-clusters are invented, and the reductionist natural vocabulary of the first books is inundated by references to science, technology, and political events. These short, usually untitled poems move along by lightning-quick flashes of intuition, and their message, as Michael Hamburger aptly puts it, 'is at once more urgent and more reticent'. One feels both a shrinking and an expansion in them, as if, by traveling to the inmost recesses of himself, Celan had somehow vanished, joining with the greater forces beyond him – and at the same time sinking more deeply into his isolation.

Thread-suns
over the gray-black wasteland.
A tree-
high thought

strikes the note of light: there are
still songs to sing beyond
mankind.
    (trans. by Joachim Neugroschel)

In poems such as this one, Celan has set the stakes so high that he must surpass himself in order to keep even with himself – and push his life into the void in order to cling to his identity. It is an impossible struggle, doomed from the start to disaster. For poetry cannot save the soul or retrieve a lost world. It simply asserts the given. In the end, it seems, Celan's desolation became too great to be borne, as if, in some sense, the world were no longer there for him. And when nothing was left, there could be no more words.

You were my death:
you I could hold
when all fell away from me.
    (trans. by Michael Hamburger)

1975

The Death of Sir Walter Ralegh

The Tower is stone and the solitude of stone. It is the skull of a man around the body of a man – and its quick is thought. But no thought will ever reach the other side of the wall. And the wall will not crumble, even against the hammer of a man's eye. For the eyes are blind, and if they see, it is only because they have learned to see where no light is. There is nothing here but thought, and there is nothing. The man is a stone that breathes, and he will die. The only thing that waits for him is death.

The subject is therefore life and death. And the subject is death. Whether the man who lives will have truly lived until the moment of his death, or whether death is no more than the moment at which life stops. This is an argument of act, and therefore an act which rebuts the argument of any word. For we will never manage to say what we want to say, and whatever is said will be said in the knowledge of this failure. All this is speculation.

One thing is sure: this man will die. The Tower is impervious, and the depth of stone has no limit. But thought nevertheless determines its own boundaries, and the man who thinks can now and then surpass himself, even when there is nowhere to go. He can reduce himself to a stone, or he can write the history of the world. Where no possibility exists, everything becomes possible again.

Therefore Ralegh. Or life lived as a suicide pact with oneself. And whether or not there is an art – if one can call it art – of living. Take everything away from a man, and this man will continue to exist. If he has been able to live, he will be able to die. And when there is nothing left, he will know how to face the wall.

It is death. And we say 'death', as if we meant to say the

thing we cannot know. And yet we know, and we know that we know. For we hold this knowledge to be irrefutable. It is a question for which no answer comes, and it will lead us to many questions that in their turn will lead us back to the thing we cannot know. We may well ask, then, what we will ask. For the subject is not only life and death. It is death, and it is life.

At each moment there is the possibility of what is not. And from each thought, an opposite thought is born. From death, he will see an image of life. And from one place, there will be the boon of another place. America. And at the limit of thought, where the new world nullifies the old, a place is invented to take the place of death. He has already touched its shores, and its image will haunt him to the very end. It is Paradise, it is the Garden before the Fall, and it gives birth to a thought that ranges farther than the grasp of any man. And this man will die. And not only will he die – he will be murdered. An axe will cut off his head.

This is how it begins. And this is how it ends. We all know that we will die. And if there is any truth we live with, it is that we die. But we may well ask the question of how and when, and we may well begin to ask ourselves if chance is not the only god. The Christian says not, and the suicide says not. Each of them says he can choose, and each of them does choose, by faith, or the lack of it. But what of the man who neither believes nor does not believe? He will throw himself into life, live life to the fullest of life, and then come to his end. For death is a very wall, and beyond this wall no one can pass. We will not ask, therefore, whether or not one can choose. One can choose and one cannot. It depends on whom and on why. To begin, then, we must find a place where we are alone and nevertheless together, that is to say, the place where we end. There is the wall, and there is the truth we confront. The question is: at what moment does one begin to see the wall?

Consider the facts. Thirteen years in the Tower, and then the final voyage to the West. Whether or not he was guilty (and he was not), has no bearing on the facts. Thirteen years in the Tower, and a man will begin to learn what solitude is. He will learn that he is nothing more than a body, and he will learn that he is nothing more than a mind, and he will learn that he is nothing. He can breathe, he can walk, he can speak, he can read, he can write, he can sleep. He can count the stones. He can be a stone that breathes, or he can write the history of the world. But at each moment he is the captive of others, and his will is no longer his own. Only his thoughts belong to him, and he is as alone with them as he is alone with the shadow he has become. But he lives. And not only does he live – he lives to the fullest that his confines will permit. And beyond them. For an image of death will nevertheless goad him into finding life. And yet, nothing has changed. For the only thing that waits for him is death.

But this is not all. And the facts must be considered still further. For the day comes when he is allowed to leave the Tower. He has been freed, but he is nevertheless not free. A full pardon will be granted only on the condition that he accomplish something that is flatly impossible to accomplish. Already the victim of the basest political intrigue, the butt of justice gone berserk, he will have his last fling and create his most magnificent failure as a sadistic entertainment for his captors. Once called the Fox, he is now like a mouse in the jaws of a cat. The King instructs him: go where the Spanish have rightful claim, rob them of their gold, and do not antagonize them or incite them to retaliation. Any other man would have laughed. Accused of having conspired with the Spanish thirteen years ago and put into the Tower as a result, he is now told to do a thing in such terms that they invalidate the very charge for which he was found guilty in the first place. But he does not laugh.

One must assume that he knew what he was doing. Either he thought that he could do what he set out to do, or the lure of the new world was so strong that he simply could not resist. In any case, it hardly matters now. Everything that could go wrong for him did go wrong, and from the very beginning the voyage was a disaster. After thirteen years of solitude, it is not easy to return to the world of men, and even less so when one is old. And he is an old man now, more than sixty, and the prison reveries in which he had seen his thoughts turn into the most glorious deeds now turn to dust before his eyes. The crew rebels against him, no gold can be found, the Spanish are hostile. Worst of all: his son is killed.

Take everything away from a man, and that man will continue to exist. But the everything of one man is not that of another, and even the strongest of men will have within himself a place of supreme vulnerability. For Ralegh, this place is occupied by his son, who is at once the emblem of his greatest strength and the seed of his undoing. To all things outward, the boy will bring doom, and though he is a child of love, he remains the living proof of lust – the wild heat of a man willing to risk everything to answer the call of his body. For this lust is nevertheless love, and such a love as seldom speaks more purely of a man's worth. For one does not cavort with a lady of the Queen unless one is ready to destroy one's position, one's honor, one's name. These women are the Queen's person, and no man, not even the most favored man, can approach or possess without royal consent. And yet, he shows no signs of contrition; he makes good on all he has done. For disgrace need not bring shame. He loves the woman, he will continue to love her, she will become the very substance of his life. And in this first, prophetic exile, his son is born.

The boy grows. And he grows wild. The father can do no more than dote and fret, prescribe warnings, be warmed by the fire of his flesh and blood. He writes an extraordinary poem of admonition to the boy, at once an ode to chance and a raging against the inevitable, telling him that if he does not mend his ways he will wind up at the end of a rope, and the boy sallies off to Paris with Ben Jonson on a colossal binge. There is nothing the father can do. It is all a question of waiting. When he is at last allowed to leave the Tower, he takes the boy along with him. He needs the comfort of his son, and he needs to feel himself the father. But the boy is murdered in the jungle. Not only does he come to the end his father had predicted for him, but the father himself has become the unwitting executioner of his own son.

And the death of the son is the death of the father. For this man will die. The journey has failed, the thought of grace does not even enter his head. England means the axe – and the gloating triumph of the King. The very wall has been reached. And yet, he goes back. To a place where the only thing that waits for him is death. He goes back when everything tells him to run for life – or to die by his own hand. For if nothing else, one can always choose one's moment. But he goes back. And the question therefore is: why cross an entire ocean only to keep an appointment with death?

We may well speak of madness, as others have. Or we may well speak of courage. But it hardly matters what we speak. For it is here that words begin to fail. And if we ever manage to say what we want to say, it will nevertheless be said in the knowledge of this failure. All this, therefore, is speculation.

If there is such a thing as an art of living, then the man who lives life as an art will have a sense of his own beginning and his own end. And beyond that, he will know that his end is in his beginning, and that each breath he draws can only bring him nearer to that end. He will live, but he will also die. For no work remains unfinished, even the one that has been abandoned.

Most men abandon their lives. They live until they do not live, and we call this death. For death is a very wall. A man dies, and therefore he no longer lives. But this does not mean it is death. For death is only in the seeing of death, and in the living of death. And we may truly say that only the man who lives his life to the fullest of life will be able to see his own death. And we may truly say what we will say. For it is here that words begin to fail.

Each man approaches the wall. One man turns his back, and in the end he is struck from behind. Another goes blind at the very thought of it and spends his life groping ahead in fear. And another sees it from the very beginning, and though his fear is no less, he will teach himself to face it, and go through life with open eyes. Every act will count, even to the last act, because nothing will matter to him anymore. He will live because he is able to die. And he will touch the very wall.

Therefore Ralegh. Or the art of living as the art of death. Therefore England – and therefore the axe. For the subject is not only life and death. It is death. And it is life. And we may truly say what we will say.

                                                            1975

Innocence and Memory

From his earliest important poems, written in the trenches of the First World War, to the last poems of his old age, Giuseppe Ungaretti's work is a long record of confrontations with death. Cryptic in utterance, narrow in range, and built on an imagery that is drawn exclusively from the natural world, Ungaretti's poetry nevertheless manages to avoid the predictable, and in spite of the limitations of his manner, he leaves an impression of almost boundless energy and invention. For no word in Ungaretti's work is ever used lightly – 'When I find / in this my silence / a word / it is dug into my life / like an abyss' – and the strength of his poetry comes precisely from this restraint. For a man who wrote for more than fifty years, Ungaretti published remarkably little before he died in 1970, and his collected poems amount to no more than a couple of hundred pages. Like Mallarmé before him (though in ways that are very different), Ungaretti's poetic source is silence, and in the end that silence is equal to the power of any word.

Born in 1888, Ungaretti belonged to a celebrated generation of modern writers that included Pound, Joyce, Kafka, Trakl, and Pessoa. Like theirs, his importance is measured not only by his own achievement but by its effect on the history of the literature of his language. Before Ungaretti, there was no modern Italian poetry. When his first book, *Il Porto Sepolto* (*The Buried Port*), appeared in 1916 in an edition of eighty copies, it seemed to have dropped from the sky, to be without precedent. These short, fragmented poems, at times hardly more ample than notes or inscriptions, announced a definitive break with the late nineteenth-century conventions that still dominated Italian poetry. The horrible realities of the war demanded a new kind of expression, and for Ungaretti, who at that time was just finishing his poetic apprenticeship, the front was a training ground that taught the futility of all compromise.

Watch
Cima Quattro, December 23, 1915

One whole night
thrust down beside
a slaughtered comrade
his snarling
mouth
turned to the full moon
the bloating
of his hands
entering
my silence
I have written
letters full of love

Never have I held
so
fast to life*

If the brevity and hardness of his first poems seemed violent in comparison to most Italian poetry of the period, Ungaretti was no poetic rebel, and his work showed none of the spirit of self-conscious sabotage that characterized the Futurists and other avant-garde groups. His break with the past was not a renunciation of literary tradition, but a way of affirming his connection with a more distant and vital past than the one represented by his immediate predecessors. He simply cleared the ground that lay between him and what he felt to be his true sources, and like all original artists, he created his own

---

*All quotations are translated by Allen Mandelbaum and appear in his *Selected Poems of Giuseppe Ungaretti*, published by Cornell University Press in 1975.

tradition. In later years, this led him to extensive critical work, as well as translations of numerous foreign poets, including Góngora, Shakespeare, Racine, Blake, and Mallarmé.

Ungaretti's need to invent this poetic past for himself can perhaps be attributed to the unusual circumstances of his early life. By the twin accidents of his birthplace and the nature of his education, he was freed from many of the constraints of a pure Italian upbringing, and though he came from old Tuscan peasant stock, he did not set foot in Italy until he was twenty-four. His father, originally from Lucca, had emigrated to Egypt to work on the construction of the Suez Canal, and by the time of Ungaretti's birth he had become the proprietor of a bakery in the Arab quarter of Moharrem Bay in Alexandria. Ungaretti attended French schools, and his first real encounter with Europe took place a year before the war, in Paris, where he met Picasso, Braque, De Chirico, Max Jacob, and became close friends with Apollinaire. (In 1918, transferred to Paris at the time of the Armistice, he arrived at Apollinaire's house with the latter's favorite Italian cigars just moments after his death.) Apart from serving in the Italian army, Ungaretti did not live in Italy until 1921 – long after he had found his direction as a poet. Ungaretti was a cultural hybrid, and elements of his varied past are continually mixed into his work. Nowhere is this more concisely expressed than in 'I fiumi' ('The Rivers') (1916), a long poem that concludes:

> I have gone over
> the seasons
> of my life
>
> These are
> my rivers
>
> This is the Serchio
> from whose waters have drawn
> perhaps two thousand years

of my farming people
and my father and my mother

This is the Nile
that saw me
born and growing
burning with unknowing
on its broad plains

This is the Seine
and in its troubled flow
I was remingled and remade
and came to know myself

These are my rivers
counted in the Isonzo

This is my nostalgia
as it appears
in each river
now it is night
now my life seems to me
a corolla
of shadows

    In early poems such as this one, Ungaretti manages to capture the past in the shape of an eternal present. Time exists, not as duration so much as accumulation, a gathering of discrete moments that can be revived and made to emerge in the nearness of the present. 'Innocence and Memory' – the title given to the French edition of Ungaretti's essays – are the two contradictory aspirations embedded in his poetry, and all his work can be seen as a constant effort to renew the self without destroying its past. What concerns Ungaretti most is the search for spiritual self-definition, a way of discovering his own essence beyond the grip of time. It is a drama played out between the forces of permanence and impermanence, and its basic fact is human mortality. As in the war poem, 'Watch', the sense of life for Ungaretti is experienced most fully in confronting death, and in a commentary on another of his poems, he describes this process as '. . . the knowing of being out of non-being, being out of the null, Pascalian knowing of being out of the null. Horrid consciousness'.

If this poetry can be described as basically religious in nature, the sensibility that informs the poems is never monkish, and denial of the flesh is never offered as a solution to spiritual problems. It is, in fact, the conflict between the spiritual and the physical that sustains the poems and gives them their life. Ungaretti is a man of contradictions, a 'man of pain', as he calls himself in one of his poems, but also a man of great passions and desires, who at times seems locked in 'the glare of promiscuity', and who is able to write of '. . . the mare of your loins / Plunging you in agony / Into my singing arms'. His obsession with death, therefore, does not derive from morbid self-pity or a search for other-worldliness, but from an almost savage will to live, and Ungaretti's robust sensuality, his firm adherence to the world of physical things, makes his poems tense with conflict between the irreconcilable powers of love and vanity.

In his later work, beginning with the second major collection, *Sentimento del Tempo* (*Sentiment of Time*) (1919–35), the distance between the present and the past grows, in the end becoming a chasm that is almost impossible to cross, either by an act of will or an act of grace. As with Pascal, as with Leopardi, the perception of the void translates itself into the central metaphor of an unappeasable agony in the face of an indifferent universe, and if Ungaretti's conversion to Catholicism in the late twenties is to be understood, it must be seen in the light of this 'horrid consciousness'. 'La Pietà' (1928), the long poem that most clearly marks Ungaretti's conversion, is also one of his bleakest works, and it contains these lines, which can be read as a gloss on the particular nature of Ungaretti's anguish:

You have banished me from life.

And will you banish me from death?

Perhaps man is unworthy even of hope.

Dry, too, the fountain of remorse?

What matters sin
If it no longer leads to purity?

The flesh can scarcely remember
That once it was strong.

Worn out and wild – the soul.

God, look upon our weakness.

We want a certainty.

Not satisfied to remain on safe ground, without the comfort of a 'certainty', he continually goads himself to the edge of the abyss, threatening himself with the image of his own extinction. But rather than inducing him to succumb to despair, these acts of metaphysical risk seem to be the source of an enduring strength. In poems such as 'The Premeditated Death', a sequence that serves as the hub to the whole of *Sentimento del Tempo*, and nearly all the poems in his following collection, *Il Dolore* (*The Grief*) (1936–47) – most notably the powerful poem written on the death of his young son, 'You Shattered' – Ungaretti's determination to situate himself at the extremes of his own consciousness is paradoxically what allows him to cure himself of the fear of these limits.

By the force and precision of his meditative insight, Ungaretti manages to transcend what in a lesser poet would amount to little more than an inventory of private griefs and fears: the poems stand as objects beyond the self for the very reason that the self within them is not treated as an example of all selves or the self in general. At all times one feels the presence of the man himself in the work. As Allen Mandelbaum notes in the preface to his translations: 'Ungaretti's I is grave and slow, intensive rather than far-ranging; and his longing gains its drama precisely because that I is not a random center of desperations, but a *soma* bound by weight, by earthly measure, a hard, resisting, substantial object, not wished but willed, not dreamt-upon but "excavated".'

In the poems of his later years, Ungaretti's work comes to an astonishing culmination in the single image of the promised land. It is the promised land of both Aeneas and the Bible, of both Rome and the desert, and the personal and historical overtones of these final major poems – 'Canzone', 'Choruses Describing the States of Mind of Dido', 'Recitative of Palinurus' and 'Final Choruses for the Promised Land' – refer back to all of Ungaretti's previous work, as if to give it its final meaning. The return to a Virgilian setting represents a kind of poetic homecoming for him at the end of his career, just as the desert revives the landscape of his youth, only to leave him in a last and permanent exile:

> We cross the desert with remnants
> Of some earlier image in mind,
>
> That is all a living man
> Knows of the promised land.

Written between 1952 and 1960, the 'Final Choruses' were published in *Il Taccuino del Vecchio* (*The Old Man's Notebook*), and they reformulate all the essential themes of his work. Ungaretti's universe remains the same, and in a language that differs very little from that of his earliest poems, he prepares himself for his death – his real death, the last death possible for him:

> The kite hawk grips me in his azure talons
> And, at the apex of the sun,

Lets me fall on the sand
As food for ravens.

I shall no longer bear mud on my shoulders,
The fire will find me clean,
The cackling beaks
The stinking jaws of jackals.

Then as he searches with his stick
Through the sand, the bedouin
Will point out
A white, white bone.

1976

Northern Lights
The paintings of Jean-Paul Riopelle

Progress of the Soul

At the limit of a man, the earth will disappear. And each thing seen of earth will be lost in the man who comes to this place. His eyes will open on earth, and whiteness will engulf the man. For this is the limit of earth – and therefore a place where no man can be.

Nowhere. As if this were a beginning. For even here, where the land escapes all witness, a landscape will emerge. That is to say: there is never nothing where a man has come, even in a place where all has disappeared. For he cannot be anywhere until he is nowhere, and from the moment he begins to lose his bearings, he will find where he is.

Therefore, he goes to the limit of earth, even as he stands in the midst of life. And if he stands in this place, it is only by virtue of a desire to be here, at the limit of himself, as if this limit were the core of another, more secret beginning of the world. For he will meet himself in his own disappearance, and in this absence he will discover the earth – even at the limit of earth.

The Body's Space

There is no need, then, except the need to be here. As if he, too, could cross into life and take his stand among the things that stand among him: a single thing, even the least thing, of all the things he is not. There is this desire, and it is inalienable. As if, by opening his eyes, he might find himself in the world.

A forest. And within that forest, a tree. And upon that tree, a leaf. A single leaf, turning in the wind. This leaf, and nothing else. The thing to be seen.

To be seen: as if he could be here. But the eye has never been enough. It cannot merely see, nor can it tell him how to see. For when a single leaf turns, it is the entire forest that turns around it. And he who turns around himself.

He wants to see what is. But no thing, not even the least thing, has ever stood still for him. For a leaf is not only a leaf: it is the earth, it is the sky, it is the tree it hangs from in the light of any given hour. But it is also a leaf. That is to say, it is what moves.

It is not enough, then, simply for him to open his eyes. If he is to see, he must begin by moving toward the thing that moves. For seeing is a process that engages the entire body. And though he begins as a witness of the thing he is not, once the first step has been taken, he becomes a participant in a motion that knows no boundaries between self and object.

Distances: what the quickness of the eye discovers, the body must then follow into experience. There is this distance to be crossed, and each time it is a new distance, a different space that opens before the eye. For no two leaves are alike. Therefore, he must feel his feet on the earth: and learn, with a patience that is the instinct of breath and blood, that this same earth is the destiny of the leaf as well.

Disappearance

He begins at the beginning. And each time he begins, it is as if he had never lived before. Painting. Or the desire to vanish in the act of seeing. That is to say: to see the thing that is, and each time to see it for the first time, as if it were the last time that he would ever see.

At the limit of himself: the pursuit of the nearly-nothing. To breathe in the whiteness of the farthest north. And all that is lost, to be born again from this emptiness in the place where desire carries him, and dismembers him, and scatters him back into earth.

For when he is here, he is nowhere. And time does not exist for him. He will suffer no duration, no continuity, no history:

time is merely an alternation between being and not being, and at the moment he begins to feel time passing within him, he knows that he is no longer alive. The self flares up in an image of itself, and the body traces a movement it has traced a thousand times before. This is the curse of memory. Or the separation of the body from the world.

If he is to begin, then, he must carry himself to a place beyond memory. For once a gesture has been repeated, once a road has been discovered, the act of living becomes a kind of death. The body must empty itself of the world in order to find the world, and each thing must be made to disappear before it can be seen. The impossible is that which allows him to breathe, and if there is life in him, it is only because he is willing to risk his life.

Therefore, he goes to the limit of himself. And at the moment he no longer knows where he is, the world can begin for him again. But there is no way of knowing this in advance, no way of predicting this miracle, and between each lapse, in each void of waiting, there is terror. And not only terror. But the death of the world in himself.

The Ends of the Earth

Lassitude and fear. The endless beginning of time in the body of a man. Blindness, in the midst of life; blindness, in the solitude of a single body. Nothing happens. Or rather, everything begins to be nothing. And the world is so far from him that in each thing he sees of the world, he finds nothing but himself.

Emptiness and immobility. For as long as it takes to kill him. Here, in the midst of life, where the very density of things seems to suffocate the possibility of life, or here, in the place where memory inhabits him. There is no choice but to leave. To lock his door behind him and set out from himself. Even to the ends of the earth.

The forest. Or a lapse in the heart of time, as if there were a place where a man could stand. Whiteness opens before him, and if he sees it, it will not be with the eye of a painter, but with the body of a man struggling for life. Gradually, all is forgotten, but not through any act of will: a man can discover the world only because he must – and for the simple reason that his life depends on it.

Seeing, therefore, as a way of being in the world. And knowledge as a force that rises from within. For after being nowhere at all, he will eventually find himself so near to the things he is not that he will almost be within them.

Relations. That is to say, the forest. He begins with a single leaf: the thing to be seen. And because there is one thing, there can be everything. But before there is anything at all, there must be desire, and the joy of a desire that propels him toward his very limit. For in this place, everything connects; and he, too, is part of this process. Therefore, he must move. And as he moves, he will begin to discover where he is.

Nature

No painting captures the spirit of natural plenitude more truly than this one. Because this painter understands that the body is what sees, that there can be no seeing without motion, he is able to carry himself across the greatest distances – and come to a place of nearness and intimacy, where each thing can be set free to be what it is.

To look at one of these paintings is to enter it: to be whirled into a field of forces that is composed not only of things, but of the motion of things – of their dislocation and their harmony. For this is a man who knows the forest, and the almost inhuman energy to be found in these canvasses does not speak of an abstract program to become-one-with-nature, but rather, more basically, of a tangible need to be present, as if life could be lived only in the fullness of this desire. As a consequence, this work does not merely re-present the natural landscape. It is a record of an encounter, a process of penetration and mutual dependence, and, as such, a portrait of a man at the limit of himself.

This is a painter who paints in the same way that he breathes. He has never sought merely to create beautiful objects, but rather, in the act of painting, to make life possible for himself. For this reason, he has always avoided facile solutions, and whenever he has found his work becoming automatic, he has stopped work altogether – for as long as it takes for him to unmemorize his work, to block his means of access to the canvas. In effect, each burst of activity is a new beginning, the fruit of a period of *un*learning the art of painting – during which time he has allowed himself to discover the world once again. His is an art of both knowledge and innocence, and the perpetual freshness of his work derives from the fact that painting is not something that he does and then divorces from himself, but a necessary struggle to gain hold of his own life and place himself in the world. It is the very substance of the man.

1976

Book of the Dead

I

During the past few years, no French writer has received more serious critical attention and praise than Edmond Jabès. Maurice Blanchot, Emmanuel Levinas, and Jean Starobinski have all written extensively and enthusiastically about his work, and Jacques Derrida has remarked, flatly and without self-consciousness, that 'in the last ten years nothing has been written in France that does not have its precedent somewhere in the texts of Jabès.' Beginning with the first volume of *Le Livre des Questions*, which was published in 1963, and continuing on through the other volumes in the series,* Jabès has created a new and mysterious kind of literary work – as dazzling as it is difficult to define. Neither novel nor poem, neither essay nor play, *The Book of Questions* is a combination of all these forms, a mosaic of fragments, aphorisms, dialogues, songs, and commentaries that endlessly move around the central question of the book: how to speak what cannot be spoken. The question is the Jewish Holocaust, but it is also the question of literature itself. By a startling leap of the imagination, Jabès treats them as one and the same:

> I talked to you about the difficulty of being Jewish, which is the same as the difficulty of writing. For Judaism and writing are but the same waiting, the same hope, the same wearing out.

---

* Le Livre de Yukel (1964), *Le Retour au Livre* (1965), *Yaël* (1967), *Elya* (1969), *Aély* (1972), *El, ou le dernier livre* (1973), which are followed by three volumes of *Le Livre des Ressemblances*. Four books are available in English, all of them admirably translated by Rosmarie Waldrop: *The Book of Questions*, *The Book of Yukel*, *Return to the Book* (Wesleyan University Press), and *Elya* (Tree Books).

The son of wealthy Egyptian Jews, Jabès was born in 1912 and grew up in the French-speaking community of Cairo. His earliest literary friendships were with Max Jacob, Paul Eluard, and René Char, and in the forties and fifties he published several small books of poetry which were later collected in *Je bâtis ma demeure* (1959). Up to that point, his reputation as a poet was solid, but because he lived outside France, he was not very well known.

The Suez Crisis of 1956 changed everything for Jabès, both in his life and in his work. Forced by Nasser's regime to leave Egypt and resettle in France – consequently losing his home and all his possessions – he experienced for the first time the burden of being Jewish. Until then, his Jewishness had been nothing more than a cultural fact, a contingent element of his life. But now that he had been made to suffer for no other reason than that he was a Jew, he had become the Other, and this sudden sense of exile was transformed into a basic, metaphysical self-description.

Difficult years followed. Jabès took a job in Paris and was forced to do most of his writing on the Métro to and from work. When, not long after his arrival, his collected poems were published by Gallimard, the book was not so much an announcement of things to come as a way of marking the boundaries between his new life and what was now an irretrievable past. Jabès began studying Jewish texts – the Talmud, the Kabbala – and though this reading did not initiate a return to the religious precepts of Judaism, it did provide a way for Jabès to affirm his ties with Jewish history and thought. More than the primary source of the Torah, it was the writings and rabbinical commentaries of the Diaspora that moved Jabès, and he began to see in these books a strength particular to the Jews, one that translated itself, almost literally, into a mode of survival. In the long interval between exile and the coming of the Messiah, the people of God had become the people of the Book. For Jabès, this meant that the Book had taken on all the weight and importance of a homeland.

The Jewish world is based on written law, on a logic of words one cannot deny.

So the country of the Jews is on the scale of their world, because it is a book . . .

The Jew's fatherland is a sacred text amid the commentaries it has given rise to . . .

At the core of *The Book of Questions* there is a story – the separation of two young lovers, Sarah and Yukel, during the time of the Nazi deportations. Yukel is a writer – described as the 'witness' – who serves as Jabès's alter ego and whose words are often indistinguishable from his; Sarah is a young woman who is shipped to a concentration camp and who returns insane. But the story is never really told, and it in no way resembles a traditional narrative. Rather, it is alluded to, commented on, and now and then allowed to burst forth in the passionate and obsessive love letters exchanged between Sarah and Yukel – which seem to come from nowhere, like disembodied voices, articulating what Jabès calls 'the collective scream . . . the everlasting scream'.

> *Sarah*: I wrote you. I write you. I wrote you. I write you. I take refuge in my words, the words my pen weeps. As long as I am speaking, as long as I am writing, my pain is less keen. I join with each syllable to the point of being but a body of consonants, a soul of vowels. Is it magic? I write his name, and it becomes the man I love . . .

And Yukel, toward the end of the book:

> And I read in you, through your dress and your skin, through your flesh and your blood. I read, Sarah, that you were mine through every word of our language, through all the wounds of our race. I read, as one reads the Bible, our history and the story which could only be yours and mine.

This story, which is the 'central text' of the book, is submitted to extensive and elusive commentaries in Talmudic fashion. One of Jabès's most original strokes is the invention of the imaginary rabbis who engage in those conversations and interpret the text with their sayings and poems. Their remarks, which most often refer to the problem of writing the book and the nature of the Word, are elliptical, metaphorical, and set in motion a beautiful and elaborate counterpoint with the rest of the work.

> 'He is a Jew,' said Reb Tolba. 'He is leaning against a wall, watching the clouds go by.'
> 'The Jew has no use for clouds,' replied Reb Jale. 'He is counting the steps between him and his life.'

Because the story of Sarah and Yukel is not fully told, because, as Jabès implies, it *cannot* be told, the commentaries are in some sense an investigation of a text that has not been written. Like the hidden God of classic Jewish theology, the text exists only by virtue of its absence.

> 'I know you, Lord, in the measure that I do not know you. For you are He who comes.'
>
> Reb Lod

What happens in *The Book of Questions*, then, is the writing of *The Book of Questions* – or rather, the attempt to write it, a process that the reader is allowed to witness in all its gropings and hesitations. Like the narrator in Beckett's *The Unnamable*, who is cursed by 'the inability to speak [and] the inability to be silent', Jabès's narrative goes nowhere but around and around itself. As Maurice Blanchot has observed in his excellent essay on Jabès: 'The writing . . . must be accomplished in the act of interrupting itself.' A typical page in *The Book of Questions* mirrors this sense of difficulty: isolated statements and paragraphs are separated by white spaces, then broken by parenthetical remarks, by italicized passages and italics within parentheses, so that the reader's eye can never grow accustomed to a single, unbroken visual field. One reads the book by fits and starts – just as it was written.

At the same time, the book is highly structured, almost architectural in its design. Carefully divided into four parts, 'At the Threshold of the Book', 'And You Shall Be in the Book', 'The Book of the Absent', and 'The Book of the Living', it is treated by Jabès as if it were a physical place, and once we cross its threshold we pass into a kind of enchanted realm, an imaginary world that has been held in suspended animation. As Sarah writes at one point: 'I no longer know where I am. I know. I am nowhere. Here.' Mythical in its dimensions, the book for Jabès is a place where the past and the present meet and dissolve into each other. There seems nothing strange about the fact that ancient rabbis can converse with a contemporary writer, that images of stunning beauty can stand beside descriptions of the greatest devastation, or that the visionary and the commonplace can coexist on the same page. From the very beginning, when the reader encounters the writer at the threshold of the book, we know that we are entering a space unlike any other.

> 'What is going on behind this door?'
> 'A book is shedding its leaves.'
> 'What is the story of the book?'
> 'Becoming aware of a scream.'
> 'I saw rabbis go in.'
> 'They are privileged readers. They come in small groups to give us their comments.'
> 'Have they read the book?'
> 'They are reading it.'
> 'Did they happen by for the fun of it?'
> 'They foresaw the book. They are prepared to encounter it.'
> 'Do they know the characters?'
> 'They know our martyrs.'
> 'Where is the book set?'
> 'In the book.'
> 'Who are you?'
> 'I am the keeper of the house.'

> 'Where do you come from?'
> 'I have wandered . . .'

The book 'begins with difficulty – the difficulty of being and writing – and ends with difficulty'. It gives no answers. Nor can any answers ever be given – for the precise reason that the 'Jew', as one of the imaginary rabbis states, 'answers every question with another question'. Jabès conveys these ideas with a wit and eloquence that often evoke the logical hairsplitting – *pilpul* – of the Talmud. But he never deludes himself into believing that his words are anything more than 'grains of sand' thrown to the wind. At the heart of the book there is nothingness.

> 'Our hope is for knowledge,' said Reb Mendel. But not all his disciples were of his opinion.
> 'We have first to agree on the sense you give to the word "knowledge",' said the oldest of them.
> 'Knowledge means questioning,' answered Reb Mendel.
> 'What will we get out of these questions? What will we get out of all the answers which only lead to more questions, since questions are born of unsatisfactory answers?' asked the second disciple.
> 'The promise of a new question,' replied Reb Mendel.
> 'There will be a moment,' the oldest disciple continued, 'when we will have to stop interrogating. Either because there will be no answer possible, or because we will not be able to formulate any further questions. So why should we begin?'
> 'You see,' said Reb Mendel: 'at the end of an argument, there is always a decisive question unsettled.'
> 'Questioning means taking the road to despair,' continued the second disciple. 'We will never know what we are trying to learn.'

Although Jabès's imagery and sources are for the most part derived from Judaism, *The Book of Questions* is not a Jewish work in the same way that one can speak of *Paradise Lost* as a Christian work. While Jabès is, to my knowledge, the first modern poet consciously to assimilate the forms and idiosyncrasies of Jewish thought, his relationship to Jewish teachings is emotional and metaphorical rather than one of strict adherence. The Book is his central image – but it is not only the Book of the Jews (the spirals of commentary around commentary in the Midrash), but an allusion to Mallarmé's ideal Book as well (the Book that contains the world, endlessly folding in upon itself). Finally, Jabès's work must be considered as part of the on-going French poetic tradition that began in the late nineteenth century. What Jabès has done is to fuse this tradition with a certain type of Jewish discourse, and he has done so with such conviction that the marriage between the two is almost imperceptible. *The Book of Questions* came into being because Jabès found himself as a writer in the act of discovering himself as a Jew. Similar in spirit to an idea expressed by Marina Tsvetaeva – 'In this most Christian of worlds / all poets are Jews' – this equation is located at the exact centre of Jabès's work, is the kernel from which everything else springs. To Jabès, nothing can be written about the Holocaust unless writing itself is first put into question. If language is to be pushed to the limit, then the writer must condemn himself to an exile of doubt, to a desert of uncertainty. What he must do, in effect, is create a poetics of absence. The dead cannot be brought back to life. But they can be heard, and their voices live in the Book.

1976

II

(The following interview with Edmond Jabès took place in Providence, Rhode Island on 4 November 1978. It was conducted in French.)

PAUL AUSTER: In the United States you are known primarily as the author of *The Book of Questions*. Few people are aware of the fact that you have also written numerous books of poetry. Readers here tend to think of you as a French writer, but in point of fact this is not strictly the case. You were born in Egypt, and it wasn't until the Suez Crisis of 1956 – when you were forty-four years old – that you moved to France. It has often occurred to me that *The Book of Questions* never would have come into being if you had been able to remain in Egypt.

EDMOND JABÈS: Yes, I think it's important to mention all this. I was born in Cairo, and except for the few years I spent in France as a student, I always lived in Egypt. I grew up in Egypt, I was married in Egypt, and I wrote poems in Egypt. In 1959, a few years after my arrival in France, Gallimard published a large collection of my poetry, *Je bâtis ma demeure*, which brought together all the little books and pamphlets I had published in Cairo and France. You say that in the United States I am known only for *The Book of Questions* . . . In France, too, I was hardly known at all, and when this big book appeared it came as something of a surprise to most people. I have always lived in the margins, so to speak . . . even though my early poems were very close to Surrealism and I had many friends who were Surrealists. Eluard, for example, was very eager for me to join the group, to participate actively in the movement. But I have always refused to join any kind of group. From the very beginning I have felt that the risks a writer takes must be taken alone. The idea of sharing these risks is upsetting to me. Something very important is taken away from you then, and as far as I'm concerned, if there is no risk, there is no writing.

PA: But as individuals the Surrealists were important to you, as individual writers.

EJ: Very important. And I felt my work was very close to theirs . . . I should say, however, that my first guide was Max Jacob. Max Jacob gave me extraordinary lessons in poetry. We met in 1935 and went on writing to each other until the war, until 1940. I really owe him a great deal. The Surrealists, as you know, were very unjust to Max because of his religious beliefs. But we are beginning to understand his importance now, to see his work as a turning-point in poetry. He was much more concerned with a questioning of language than the others in his circle. Apollinaire, for example, was a great lyric poet, a poet of pure singing, but Max was something else altogether, and there is a very moving quality in the way he questions language. Everyone thought of him as a clown, as someone who played with puns, jokes, and linguistic tricks, but that wasn't so. It only looked that way on the surface. Underneath, Max was an extremely tortured, anguished person . . . As for the Surrealists, of course, they had an enormous influence on my work. But even so, there were important differences. When I look back on my early poems now, I am struck by what they seem to foreshadow of *The Book of Questions*. In the aphorisms, for example, although I had no idea at the time . . . But, as you say, I don't think I would have written *The Book of Questions* if I had remained in Egypt. It took this break in my life for my experience of Egypt, my experience of the desert, to enter my writing in the way it does. These books came into being as a result of this break . . . as a result of my having to leave this country because I was a Jew. One day I was told, this is it, you have to leave. Fine. This was a little drama for me and my family. On a personal level it was quite serious, of course, but on the larger, human scale, as part of the history of Jewish suffering, it was nothing more than a little drama. But there I was, neither a practising Jew nor a Jewish believer, forced to leave because I was Jewish.

PA: Were you brought up in a religious family?

EJ: No. Our family was very bourgeois. We always considered ourselves Jews, but nothing more. My father did not really believe in God, and he observed very few Jewish practices. We were brought up in an atmosphere of total freedom.

PA: And you weren't given any kind of Jewish education?

EJ: No, none whatsoever. But the fact of suddenly having to live a condition, the condition of being Jewish, changed things for me. I was faced with new problems, and this led to a completely new kind of questioning for me. In some sense this was the origin of the series of books that followed.

PA: Long before the Suez Crisis, of course, there was the war. The situation of the Jews in Europe during that time needs no elaboration from us here today. But the situation in Egypt, on the other hand, is not so well known.

EJ: It was dramatic, as it was everywhere else. But a certain category of the population . . . the native Egyptian population, was neither for the Allies nor for the Germans. The leaders of the country were pro-German because of the Turkish origins of the royal family. But Egypt was also occupied by the English at that time, and in some way, even though we knew the war was going on, we didn't feel it. The war didn't become real for us until Rommel's advance. At that point I became quite active . . . and eventually went to Palestine with the British troops. I stayed there nine months. It was only then that we truly became aware of all that was at stake in the war. We understood what the consequences would be if the Germans won . . . But still, we weren't forced to live the situation as people in Europe were forced to live it. There was no German occupation for us, no one was deported . . . in some sense we were protected by the English. As early as 1935, however, we were given some idea of the atrocities of the camps from the Jewish refugee boats that stopped at Port Said; we saw women whose arms and necks had been burned by cigars and cigarettes, and people told us quite a bit about what was going on. Along with many others, I was very active in protesting the rise of Nazism. There were many marches and demonstrations . . . but that doesn't mean we were directly affected by what was happening.

PA: You could almost say that your situation was similar to that of the American Jews. You were aware of what was taking place, but you weren't immediately threatened by it.

EJ: Yes, that's it exactly. That's a very good comparison . . . In Egypt, things didn't begin to deteriorate until the war was over. After the declaration of the State of Israel in 1948, the situation of the Jews became very bad. The propaganda attacks began. At first they were against the 'Zionists', but very quickly the word 'Zionists' was replaced by the word 'Jew'. The people, the Egyptian people, weren't really aware of what was happening. When they were called on to demonstrate or to attack and burn Jewish stores, of course, they did it, but only because they were living in great misery and it was almost an officially approved way for them to vent their frustrations. But I can't really say that the poor people were deeply anti-Semitic. It was the intellectuals and the students who led the attack . . . mixing up very confused ideas about Marxism, Nazism, and a whole salad of other things. The Jews were naturally the first to be attacked because Israel was considered the enemy of the whole Middle East, of all the Arab countries. Since the Arab countries were not able to get along among themselves, Israel became a convenient scapegoat. And little by little all Jews became

Israelis in their minds . . . the distinctions were no longer made. With each war, the situation became worse. By 1956, it was no longer possible to remain.

PA: Were you tempted by the idea of Israel? Between 1948 and 1956, for example, did you ever think of moving there?

EJ: No, never. I've never thought of Israel as a solution to the problem. It's not that I'm against Israel . . . quite the contrary. But I think it's wrong to consider it as the one and only answer . . . There is the Israel of Jewish history, the age-old dream of Israel, and there is the State of Israel, which is one country among all the other countries in the world today. They are not the same.

PA: France, then, became the inevitable choice.

EJ: It was inevitable because French is my language, the language of my books. I was very warmly welcomed in France by everyone. But it would be impossible for me to say that France is my country, that it is my landscape . . . I feel a little lost living in Paris, even though I am surrounded by friends and feel comfortable there. It is not my landscape, not my place, my true place. In a sense, I am now living out the historical Jewish condition. The book has become my true place . . . practically my only place. This idea has become very important to me, to such an extent, in fact, that the condition of being a writer has little by little become almost the same for me as the condition of being a Jew. I feel that every writer in some way experiences the Jewish condition, because every writer, every creator, lives in a kind of exile. And for the Jew himself, the Jew living out the Jewish condition, the book has become not only the place where he can most easily find himself, but also the place where he finds his truth. And the questioning of the book for the Jew, as you know, is a search for the truth. And this truth is also the writer's truth. When the writer questions the book, it is solely in order to enter the truth of the book, which is his truth.

PA: How exactly did these ideas take shape for you?

EJ: Actually, it's quite curious. When I came to France I had fourteen years of poetry behind me, and when the book came out I was naturally very happy about it. But at the same time, I felt that a part of my life was over, that a page had been turned. It was as if I were reliving the experience of the desert . . . as if I had suddenly come to a blank page . . . In Egypt I had written some pieces for the theater, and I thought to myself that perhaps this was the sort of writing I would do now. The work that I was later to call *The Book of Questions* came to me very slowly . . . at first in the form of a drama that took on more and more symbolic importance, and then in the form of reflections that had no definite shape. It was all very vague. Eventually I realized that this had nothing to do with the theater. But if it wasn't theater, what was it? Little by little, as if in spite of me, this thing began to emerge, the book I had been pursuing in total darkness began to take shape . . . by means of questioning, by means of a dramatic story I wanted to present in the same way I felt it inside me, a story I wanted to tell without ever really telling it. It was as if there were stories that didn't have to be told in order to be known and understood. And this was something quite new in a formal sense: that wasn't the way you were supposed to tell a story. But the idea of a story in itself didn't satisfy me . . . that really wasn't what I was after. But around the story I had in mind, there was the questioning, and more and more that became what haunted me about the book. It was as if the book would be something in which I could at last find myself, in which I would find my universe, as if the book were about to become some fantastic thing in which a whole adventure was going to begin.

PA: Were the rabbis already present when you were thinking of the work in terms of the theater?

EJ: No, there were characters. But they became rabbis for the book, because, as you know, rabbis are interpreters, the best interpreters of the book. And once the rabbis were there, I needed a whole crowd of them. The nature of the questioning demanded it. You can't say black and white at the same time; you need one to say white and another to say black . . . Perhaps it would be best to explain this in terms of overall structure.

PA: By all means.

EJ: In the first trilogy – *The Book of Questions, The Book of Yukel,* and *Return to the Book* – the references to Judaism are very marked. At the center of each of these books there is a story, the story of two adolescents . . . two lovers who are deported. They return from the camps: she has gone mad, and her cries become indistinguishable from the cries of a persecuted people, a people persecuted over the centuries; in the second volume he commits suicide, and everything takes place as if after his death. But this after-death is also a before-death . . . like memory, as if there were always something before. Then the rabbis come . . . to reflect, to question, and so on. But it's not exactly that. It is an immense dialogue in time and outside of time. And these people who are there, sometimes separated by many centuries, can speak to each other only in the form of questions.

PA: Why is that?

EJ: Because – and it was Blanchot who noticed this . . . in an article for the *NRF* published in 1964 – because when two people talk, one of them must always remain silent. We are talking now, for example, and as I am saying these words you are forced to remain silent. If we both spoke at the same time, neither one of us could hear what the other was saying. Now, during this silence that you impose on yourself, you are all the while forming questions and answers in your mind, since you can't keep interrupting me. And as I continue to speak, you are eliminating questions from your mind: ah, you say to yourself, that's what he meant, all right. But what if I went on speaking for a long time and we went away before you had a chance to reply? When we met again, you wouldn't come back with an answer, you would come back with a question. This is the way the rabbis answer each other. Each one has already eliminated the questions, and so he is able to say: this is what I think. They are not always asking questions, then, sometimes they give answers. But this answer immediately provokes a question from someone else. The whole book operates in this manner. A first dialogue is interrupted, then a second dialogue, then a third, a fourth . . . and suddenly, the first dialogue, which seemed to have been lost, is picked up again fifty pages later after a thousand other things have happened.

PA: It took you three or four years to write *The Book of Questions*.

EJ: Yes. I worked on it from 1959 to 1962, and it was published in 1963. But, as I said before, I was working in total darkness. And when the book appeared, no one really knew what to make of it. The idea of the *récit éclaté* [fragmented story] had never been discussed in France at that time, and that was how the book demanded to be read . . . demands to be read. There is a story, but it is given only in little pieces, and there are the two characters, Sarah and Yukel – but Yukel is double. He is both the narrator (the one who makes the book) and the hero. But they are the same, they have the same name. And then, there is no place, the book isn't situated anywhere, since there are all these characters who come from various times. The rabbis – they are imaginary rabbis, of course . . . there are both ancient and modern rabbis. The most ancient rabbis are the ones who say the simplest things, and the rabbis closest to us in time say the most complicated things . . . And then, too, there are the different kinds of typography in the book . . . the parentheses and italics, for example. In all my books there is a book that exists inside the book. There is the part that is before the book . . . it is in the book, but it is also the book that has not yet been written. To be before the book is to be in a state of potential, to have the possibility of creating a book. But then the book creates itself, against all the other books we carry inside us. And it goes on and on like that. It is a circular work. Each question leads to another question.

PA: The typographical layout of your books is one of the things that most immediately strike the reader . . . It sets the rhythm of the work and enhances the feeling of fragmentation you create in the text itself. Are these shifts done in a systematic way, or are they more or less unconscious?

EJ: Sometimes it just happens, but more often than not it requires real work. It's not premeditated in the beginning, but as the text advances, there are things that come from farther and farther away, as if from another book, or from the book within the book . . . and these are the things in italics. The longer passages generally belong to the book itself, to the book that is being written, and they are there to continue the story, or to continue the questioning . . . But the material in italics is also a book being created at the same time the other book is being created. There is always a book carrying a book carrying a book carrying a book . . . As for this distribution of long and short passages, it's a question of rhythm. This is very important to me. A full phrase, a lyrical phrase, is something that has great breath, that allows you to breathe very deeply. There are other times when the work folds in on itself, and the breath becomes shorter, breathing becomes difficult. They say that Nietzsche wrote aphorisms, for example, because he suffered from atrocious headaches that made it impossible for him to write very much at any one sitting. Whether this is true or not, I do believe that a writer works with his body. You live with your body, and the book is above all the book of your body. In my case, the aphorism – what you might call the naked phrase – comes from a need to surround the words with whiteness in order to let them breathe. As you know, I suffer from asthma, and sometimes breathing is very difficult for me. By giving breath to my words I often have the feeling that I am helping myself breathe. It's really quite incredible how you live with your writing . . . I remember something that happened a few years ago. I had just finished the seven *Books of Questions* . . . it was in April. May is usually the month when my asthma is worst, but this time May came and went and I hardly had any trouble at all. June came, and I still felt fine. My doctor, who happens to be an old friend, was at my house one day, and I told him what a curious thing it was that I should be feeling so well at that time of year. He answered that perhaps it was because I had finished the series and the anguish of the work had temporarily lifted . . . A little later I went off on vacation – to the sea, where I am always fine – and returned to Paris in September, which is usually a good month for me. At that point my publisher called me and asked me to write a *prière d'insérer* [a note for the back of the book]. This kind of note is usually a bother to do, often quite difficult . . . but after two or three days I managed to get it done. The last sentence of the note was: 'With this book, the seventh in the series, *The Book of Questions* comes to an end.' That night I had one of my most violent asthma attacks. And it was the phrase 'comes to an end' that brought it on. It had thrown me into a terrible panic. The doctor had come at three in the morning to give me a shot. I almost literally couldn't breathe . . . If I say all this, it is only to show that we work with our bodies, our breathing, our rhythm, and that writing in some sense mimes all this. Writing works in two directions. It is both an expansion and a contraction. This is what I learned from Max Jacob, and it took me a long time to understand it. When I was very young, nineteen, twenty, I would send him my poems, and he would write back saying they were too broad, I should tighten them up. So I would tighten them up, and he would write back saying they are too tight, I should broaden them. I was totally confused. It took me a long time to understand that *both* were valid, but that this was what style was all about, that this was the essence of writing. You have to write in the same way you breathe.

PA: You once told me that as you were writing *The Book of Questions* you had the feeling that you were taking dictation.

EJ: Not quite . . . but almost. A great part of it, as you know, was written on the metro going to and from work, and of course there were a lot of people around. It was as if . . . as if something had imposed this book on me. But I do not believe in inspiration, or anything like it. The book emerged from something that was already deeply inside me.

PA: Were your early poems written in this way? Or did something truly different begin for you with *The Book of Questions*?

EJ: There is something that always intrigued me about writing poems . . . which is that I could always say how long a poem would be even before I wrote it. I knew if it was going to be three pages, or six pages, or half a page . . . The only way this can be explained, I think, is by the fact that when you begin writing a poem it has already been written within you, even though you are not aware of it. It was all very curious for me. I could begin writing a poem, for example, put down a phrase or two, and then go out, say to the movies, anywhere, and know that when I returned home I would be able to continue writing. Without for one minute having been separated from the poem. As if it had continued working inside me. I remember a long poem of ten pages. One evening I came home and went to bed. In the middle of the night I got up. My wife said, what's going on, are you ill? I said no, I'm going to write. And I sat down at my desk and began to write this poem. After a while I went back to bed. The next day I picked up as if I had never left it. Going back to bed, I said to my wife: this is a poem that will be ten pages long. And it turned out to be ten pages, exactly. How can you explain this? It's incomprehensible. Something is already at work inside us and then some little thing, an emotion, a chance encounter, sets it off . . . That's why the dry stretches in poetry are particularly painful, the times when you can't write anything. You're going along very well. You write ten poems, twenty poems in just a few months, and you feel wonderful. And then, suddenly, you can't do a thing. You can't even pick up your pen, you can't write a line. At those times you are filled with terrible doubt. You are afraid you might never be able to write again. This is something extraordinary, something most people don't understand. Whenever you write you are running the risk of never writing again . . . And then, sometimes, a new poem comes, and you feel completely liberated. You say to yourself, at last, it's come back. And you write and write, and in the end you discover that it doesn't amount to anything . . . Writing comes in its own time . . . you can never force it.

PA: Concerning the narrative element in *The Book of Questions* . . . the fragmentary nature of the telling. Is it a matter of choice, or do you somehow find it impossible to tell a story in the traditional way?

EJ: It is neither a choice nor an impossibility. To tell a story, in my opinion, is to lose it. If I tell you about my life in detail, for example, it escapes in the details I have chosen to recount. In life you have no choice. How do you know what is most important? A story limits the life of a person to the things someone else can say about him. He is big, he is small, he is this, he is that. Even if all this is true, there is still something else. But if I say: he was born here, he died here, a whole life begins to take shape, a life that you might be able to imagine . . .

PA: What you are saying, then, is that the traditional narrative doesn't interest you.

EJ: . . . *The Book of Questions* is based on the idea that we all live with words that obsess us. There is no question that highly emotional words such as 'death' or 'love', for example, do not have precisely the same meanings for everyone. Behind these words we see our own stories of death and love. As for the story in the book, I simply wanted to point out the life and drama of this couple. It was not a question of telling the story of their lives, because in the end it wasn't their lives that interested me . . . I am more concerned with interiority than description. It is the questioning around the story that gives the story its dimension. But the story is there only as a kind of basic pretext. For the Jews unfortunately, after all the camps and all the horrors, it is an all too banal story. It isn't necessary to go into details. When you say: they were deported, that is enough for a Jew to understand the *whole* story . . . I once met a man who had lost his whole family in the camps. Only he and his son had escaped. He told me this and then went on to talk about completely different kinds of things. I felt that he had told me his *whole* life, past, present, and even future by simply saying to me: 'My whole family was deported. Only my son and I escaped.' This conversation made a particularly deep impression on me because the man later went on to tell me about his son. During the blockade of Jerusalem, when the Syrians were firing on the supply trucks going to the city, the son, who was only fifteen or sixteen at the time, asked his father permission to become a driver of one of these condemned trucks. The father said yes. And the boy was killed. And after that the father took his son's name. His name was Ben Zvi, and it was because I asked him about his name that he told me the story. It is something I will never forget . . . And it shows, I think, that it is enough simply to tell the thing in order to reveal the whole drama.

PA: You spoke of obsessive words. There are a dozen or so words and themes that are repeated constantly, on nearly every page of your work: desert, absence, silence, God, nothingness, the void, the book, the word, exile, life, death . . . and it strikes me that each of these words is in some sense a word on the other side of speech, a kind of limit, something almost impossible to express.

EJ: Exactly. But at the same time, if these are things that cannot be expressed, they are also things that cannot be emptied of meaning. We can't get rid of them. I find it impossible to rid myself of the word 'Jew', for example, or the word 'God'. This created considerable misunderstanding in the beginning. Why God, people asked, when you don't believe in God? There are people in France, you know, people who call themselves materialists, who are afraid of saying words like 'God'. I find this idiotic. The word 'God' is in the dictionary, it's a word like any other word. I am not afraid of the word 'God', because I am not afraid of this God . . . What I mean by God in my work is something we come up against, an abyss, a void, something against which we are powerless. It is a distance . . . the distance that is always between things . . . We get to where we are going, and then there is still this distance to cover. And a moment comes when you can no longer cover the distance; you get there and you say to yourself, it's finished, there are no more words. God is perhaps a word without words. A word without meaning. And the extraordinary thing is that in the Jewish tradition God is invisible, and as a way of underscoring this invisibility, he has an unpronounceable name. What I find truly fantastic is that when you call something 'invisible', you are naming something, which means that you are almost giving a representation of the invisible. In other words, when you say 'invisible', you are pointing to the boundary between the visible and the invisible; there are words for that. But when you can't say the word, you are standing before nothing. And for me this is even more powerful because, finally, there is a visible in the invisible, just as there is an invisible in the visible. And this, this abolishes everything.

PA: In a sense, all these words become the same word, and they end up destroying each other.

EJ: They destroy each other in the questioning of themselves, in the process of moving towards the void. At one point I wrote: 'the truth is perhaps this void', meaning whatever it is that stands at the limit of truth. There is a constant effacement, a constant peeling of layers, a stripping away of the name until this name becomes an unpronounceable name . . . This has nothing to do with nihilism, even though certain people have accused me of nihilism. It is the very nature of my work . . . This constant questioning of things in order to say, finally, what is identity? What are we? What is the name? This name that we bear with us, what is it? . . . I don't presume to have any answers, I ask questions. If I give a special status to the question, that is because I find something unsatisfactory about the nature of the answer. It can never completely contain us. Also, and this is quite important, I feel that answers embody a certain form of power. Whereas the question is a form of non-power. But a subversive kind of non-power, one . . . that will be upsetting to power. Power does not like discussions. Power affirms, and it has only friends or enemies. Whereas the question is in between . . . A young student who was writing a paper on my books once asked me if there was any lesson to be drawn from my work. I answered: none whatsoever. It seems to me that if these books tell the reader anything, it is that he should take on the burden of what troubles him, that he should carry on his questioning to the very end. Which means putting oneself in question, doesn't it? To the very end.

PA: Which means, in other words, that it is endless.

EJ: Yes, there is no end to it. There are some people, of course, who eventually find some kind of peace . . . But I have never found this peace. It seems that I am someone compelled to ask questions. And in my books, everything truly important or essential to me, I think, has been called into question. After the first trilogy of *The Book of Questions* – in which the references to Judaism are very marked – the next two books *Yaël* and *Elya* deal with the relationship between the writer and his words. It becomes more and more personal . . . The series, which continues on through *Aély*, ends with *El*, which is a point, *El, ou le dernier livre* [the last book]. The point, or the dot, is on the cover of the book and is actually the title. It is the smallest possible circle, the circle that has become a dot, or a period, the circle within the circle. In the Kabbala it says, 'God reveals himself in a dot', and by making this reference, the whole work of deconstruction seems to uncover a totality. But this totality can never be shown. Totality is an idea . . . and it can be shown only through fragments . . . For example, we are in this room and cannot see the whole house. But we know that we are in the house. The same thing happens in the book. We know that we are in something immense, but at each moment we can only see what is in front of us . . . Totality is something we reconstitute ourselves through all these fragments, because these fragments are what provides visibility. In the same way, a book can be read because of the words. It is the word which allows us to read the book, not the book which allows us to read the word. The book, of course, is the place in which the word evolves, but as we move on, it is the word, the word in this void, in this space between one word and the next, that makes it possible to read. Our reading takes place in the very whiteness between the words, for this whiteness reminds us of the much greater space in which the word evolves.

PA: In speaking of 'the word', of course, we are running into something of a translation problem. In French there is a clear distinction between *parole* and *mot*, whereas in English we have only 'word'. It is the difference between speaking and writing.

EJ: That is why I always use the word *vocable*. In English it must be a little difficult. 'Vocable'? That sounds a bit heavy. In French, too, however, it is not a common word . . . One of the fundamental differences between the written and spoken word is that the written word can be seen. Speaking is more limited. One cannot speak about what will happen, only about what has already happened. In writing, however, you find yourself before something that is about to begin. You enter into another time, another world . . . into something that will express us, although you don't know exactly what it is. This is the reason for all my reticence concerning literary theory. I discuss many theoretical questions in these books, of course, but I never begin with theory *a priori*. Literature for me is a real adventure, and if things are already mapped out for you in advance, how can there be any adventure? You are always at the beginning . . . and each of my books in some way is the beginning of another book that is never written. That is why when the second book prolongs the first, it also cancels out part of the reading you have already made.

PA: They cancel out, in the same way the words cancel each other out.

EJ: Yes. They cancel out the reading so that you can make another reading. And this process keeps repeating itself, endlessly . . . Someone was talking about Mallarmé's book the other day . . . but I think there is an enormous difference between what I call the book and Mallarmé's book. Mallarmé wanted to put all knowledge into a book. He wanted to make a great book, the book of books. But in my opinion this book would be very ephemeral, since knowledge in itself is ephemeral. The book that would have a chance to survive, I think, is the book that destroys itself. That destroys itself in favor of another book that will prolong it. This is the point, if you will, of my deconstruction of the book.

PA: It remains open, whereas Mallarmé's book folds in on itself and remains closed.

EJ: Exactly. It all takes place because of the nature of the questioning. It is a matter of saying at each moment, that isn't enough, I have to go farther. This leads to something else, which in turn must be questioned . . . The book carries all books within itself, and each fragment is the beginning of the book, the book that is created within the book and which at the same time is taken apart. It is lost at the same time it comes into being . . . just as we lose ourselves in the child we create, since the child will eventually replace us . . . As you can see, this attitude is very different from one that says: we do not exist, I obliterate myself, thank you and goodbye. No. I efface myself in order to go even farther.

PA: You have written somewhere that writing has nothing to do with imagination. This is a rather provocative statement, and I wonder if you could elaborate on it.

EJ: I don't imagine anything. I am carried along by the word [*vocable*] itself, by the questioning of the word. The progress of the book is what allows me to move ahead. It has nothing to do with inventing, with saying that I am going to imagine such and such and question it in this way. No. It's similar to what we are doing now. We're speaking, and it's you who are giving me the questions. I'm not imagining anything at all . . . It has to do with experience, with having lived something, rather than imagination. In Boulder a girl came up to me and said she had been struck by the sentence, 'When I was twelve years old, I lost the sky.' Why not ten years old, she asked, or fifteen, or why not simply 'When I was a child'? Why does it have to be twelve? This was an excellent question. Twelve, as it turns out, was a very important age for me. When I was twelve years old my sister died in my arms . . . and this was something that marked me for life. You can see, then, that behind each thing there is a background of experience, something that has been lived in the past and that touches me deeply.

PA: Another important element in your work, especially in the more recent books – I'm thinking of *Aély* and *El* – is an almost constant playing with words, sounds, letters, meanings . . . The word *sol* [land], for example, which you detach from the word *solitude*, which in turn summons the word *solacier* [to console] . . . as if the whole range of feelings and ideas could be evoked in the simple act of breaking up a word.

EJ: I have tried to question the book on all its levels . . . In *El*, the last book, there is a great deal of what I call an examination of the surface. All my books are about cutting, about disjunction. From one end to the other the book is fragmented, cut up constantly . . . and in the last book I also wanted to show how this works on the level of the word itself. I have nothing against word play. Quite the contrary. I consider it to be something very important. Only for me it is *not* just play. It is a way of getting from one place to another, a way of advancing by means of the word itself . . . In the very center of *El*, for example – on page 63 in a book of 126 pages, in other words, exactly in the middle – there is a chart with 'nul' [nothing] on the top and 'l'un' [one] on the bottom. The whole work, in effect, takes place in this 'one' and is finally cancelled out to become this 'nothing'. This reveals the essence of the fragmentation, and in some way this chart is an image of all my books . . . This work of cutting is at the very heart of the writing, at the very heart of writing itself. Why? Because in words there are things that attract and repel each other . . . Tensions and relationships arise from the fact that they have the same letters, or because there is some kind of sonority or assonance . . . And this working of word with word can only be explored by means of the word itself, not by means of anything else . . . This is the way everything in my book functions. One passage of particular importance to me, as you know, is where I say that the Hebrew people gave Moses a crucial lesson in reading when they forced him to break the tablets of the law. Because they were not able to accept a word without origins, the word of God. It was necessary for Moses to break the book in order for the book to become human . . . This gesture on the part of the Hebrew people was necessary before they could accept the book. This is exactly what we do as well. We destroy the book when we read it in order to make it into another book. The book is always born from a broken book. And the word, too, is born from a broken word.

PA: What you are saying is that this metamorphosing of words has nothing to do with playing or with magic. It is a completely conscious act.

EJ: Absolutely. If there is anything conscious about what I do, it is in this work with words.

PA: Is it a method?

EJ: No, I'm not suggesting a method . . .

PA: I mean a personal method, a means of arriving at a certain kind of reflection.

EJ: Yes. But I'm not proposing it to others. It works for me, but it might not be valid for someone else . . . I have always worked on this principle . . . which is something one of the rabbis in my next book says: do not hesitate to question the book, even those things about it which might seem absurd to others. Because everything can hide within itself a certain truth . . . What I try to do is to show that behind each word other words are hiding. And each time you change a word or make a word emerge from another word, you change the whole book. When I say there are many books in the book, it is because there are many words in the word. Obviously, if you change the word, the context of the sentence changes completely. In this way another sentence is born from this word, and a completely different book begins . . . I think of this in terms of the sea, in the image of the sea as it breaks upon the shore. It is not the wave that comes, it is the *whole* sea that comes each time and the *whole* sea that draws back. It is never just a wave, it is always everything that comes and everything that goes. This is really the fundamental movement in all my books. Everything is connected to everything else. There is the whole questioning of the ocean, in its depths, in its movement, in the foam it leaves behind, in the delicate lace it leaves upon the shore . . . At each moment, in the least question, it is the *whole* book which returns and the *whole* book which draws back.

PA: In a sense, the project is inexhaustible by definition. Each book gives birth to the next.

EJ: Yes . . . Or at least, I am incapable of abandoning it. Because the book I am going to do is never the book I want to do. If I could do the book I carry inside me, it would be the last book. And this book is impossible. If I write, it is because there is always this book I want to do over again.

PA: Earlier, we were talking about Beckett, and I'm reminded now of something he wrote in the late forties: 'To be an artist is to fail, as no other dares fail . . .'

EJ: That's a very beautiful statement. It's very beautiful . . . and that's it, exactly.

PA: It seems to me that you have been saying more or less the same thing.

EJ: Absolutely. That's it, exactly.

The Decisive Moment

Charles Reznikoff is a poet of the eye. To cross the threshold of his work is to penetrate the prehistory of matter, to find oneself exposed to a world in which language has not yet been invented. Seeing, in his poetry, always comes before speech. Each poetic utterance is an emanation of the eye, a transcription of the visible into the brute, unciphered code of being. The act of writing, therefore, is not so much an ordering of the real as a discovery of it. It is a process by which one places oneself between things and the names of things, a way of standing watch in this interval of silence and allowing things to be seen – as if for the first time – and henceforth to be given their names. The poet, who is the first man to be born, is also the last. He is Adam, but he is also the end of all generations: the mute heir of the builders of Babel. For it is he who must learn to speak from his eye – and cure himself of seeing with his mouth.

The poem, then, not as a telling, but as a taking hold. The world can never be assumed to exist. It comes into being only in the act of moving towards it. *Esse est percipii*: no American poet has ever adhered so faithfully to the Berkeleyan formula as Reznikoff. It is more than just the guiding principle of his work – it is *embedded* in the work, and it contains all the force of a moral dogma. To read Reznikoff is to understand that nothing can be taken for granted: we do not find ourselves in the midst of an already established world, we do not, as if by preordained birthright, automatically take possession of our surroundings. Each moment, each thing, must be *earned*, wrested away from the confusion of inert matter by a steadiness of gaze, a purity of perception so intense that the effort, in itself, takes on the value of a religious act. The slate has been wiped clean. It is up to the poet to write his own book.

Tiny poems, many of them barely a sentence long, make up the core of Reznikoff's work. Although his total output includes fiction, biography, drama, long narrative poems, historical meditations, and book-length documentary poems, these short lyrics are the Ur-texts of Reznikoff's imagination: everything else follows from them. Notable for their precision and simplicity, they also run counter to normal assumptions about what a poem should aspire to be. Consider these three examples:

April

The stiff lines of the twigs
blurred by buds.

Moonlit Night

The trees' shadows lie in black pools in the lawns.

The Bridge

In a cloud bones of steel.

The point is that there is no point. At least not in any traditional sense. These poems are not trying to drum home universal truths, to impress the reader with the skill of their making, or to invoke the ambiguities of human experience. Their aim, quite simply, is clarity. Of seeing and of speaking. And yet, the unsettling modesty of these poems should not blind us to the boldness of their ambition. For even in these tiniest of poems, the gist of Reznikoff's poetics is there. It is as much an ethics of the poetic moment as it is a theory of writing, and its message never varies in any of Reznikoff's work: the poem is always more than just a construction of words. Art, then, for the sake of something – which means that art is almost an incidental by-product of the effort to make it. The poem, in all instances, must be an effort to perceive, must be a moving *outward*. It is less a mode of expressing the world than it is a way of being in the world. Merleau-Ponty's account of contemplation in *The Phenomenology of Perception* is a nearly exact description of the process that takes place in a Reznikoff poem:

> . . . when I contemplate an object with the sole intention of watching it exist and unfold its riches before my eyes, then it ceases to be an allusion to a general type, and I become aware that each perception, and not merely that of sights which I am discovering for the first time, re-enacts on its own account the birth of intelligence and has some element of creative genius about it: in order that I may recognize the tree as a tree, it is necessary that, beneath this familiar meaning, the momentary arrangement of the visible scene should begin all over again, as on the very first day of the vegetable kingdom, to outline the individual idea of this tree.

Imagism, yes. But only as a source, not as a method. There is no desire on Reznikoff's part to use the image as a medium for transcendence, to make it quiver ineffably in some ethereal realm of the spirit. The progress from symbolism to imagism to objectivism is more a series of short circuits than a direct lineage. What Reznikoff learned from the Imagists was the value – the force – of the image in itself, unadorned by the claims of the ego. The poem, in Reznikoff's hands, is an act of image-ing rather than of imagining. Its impulse is away from metaphor and into the tangible, a desire to take hold of what is rather than what is merely possible. A poem fit to the measure of the perceived world, neither larger than this world nor smaller than it. 'I see something,' Reznikoff stated in a 1968 interview with L. S. Dembo, 'and I put it down as I see it. In the treatment of it, I abstain from comment. Now, if I've done something that moves me – if I've portrayed the object well – somebody will come along and also be moved, and somebody else will come along and say, "What the devil is this?" And maybe they're both right.'

If the poet's primary obligation is to see, there is a similar though less obvious injunction upon the poet – the duty of not being seen. The Reznikoff equation, which weds seeing to invisibility, cannot be made except by renunciation. In order to see, the poet must make himself invisible. He must disappear, efface himself in anonymity.

> I like the sound of the street –
> but I, apart and alone,
> beside an open window
> and behind a closed door.

*

> I am alone –
> and glad to be alone;
> I do not like people who walk about
> so late; who walk slowly after midnight
> through the leaves fallen on the sidewalks.
> I do not like
> my own face
> in the little mirrors of the slot-machines
> before the closed stores.

It seems no accident that most Reznikoff poems are rooted in the city. For only in the modern city can the one who sees remain unseen, take his stand in space and yet remain transparent. Even as he becomes a part of the landscape he has entered, he continues to be an outsider. Therefore, objectivist. That is to say – to create a world around oneself by seeing as a stranger would. What counts is the thing itself, and the thing that is seen can come to life only when the one who sees it has disappeared. There can never be any movement toward possession. Seeing is the effort to create presence: to possess a thing would be to make it vanish.

And yet, it is *as if* each act of seeing were an attempt to establish a link between the one who sees and the thing that is seen. *As if* the eye were the means by which the stranger could find his place in the world he has been exiled to. For the building of a world is above all the building and recognition of relations. To discover a thing and isolate it in its singularity is only a beginning, a first step. The world is not merely an accumulation, it is a process – and each time the eye enters this world, it partakes in the life of all the disparate things that pass before it. While objectivity is the premise, subjectivity is the tacit organizer. As soon as there is more than one thing, there is memory, and because of memory, there is language: what is born in the eye, and nevertheless beyond it. In which, and out of which, the poem.

In his 1968 interview with Dembo, Reznikoff went on to say: 'The world is very large, I think, and I certainly can't testify to the whole of it. I can only testify to my own feelings; I can only say what I saw and heard, and I try to say it as well as I can. And if your conclusion is that what I saw and heard makes you feel the way I did, then the poem is successful.'

New York was Reznikoff's home. It was a city he knew as intimately as a woodcutter knows his forest, and in his prime he would walk between ten and twenty miles a day, from Brooklyn to Riverdale and back. Few poets have ever had such a deep feeling for city life, and in dozens of brief poems Reznikoff captures the strange and transitory beauties of the urban landscape.

> This smoky winter morning –
> do not despise the green jewel among the twigs
> because it is a traffic light.
>
> *
>
> Feast, you who cross the bridge
> this cold twilight
> on these honeycombs of light, the buildings of Manhattan.
>
> *
>
> Rails in the subway,
> what did you know of happiness
> when you were ore in the earth;
> now the electric lights shine upon you.

But Reznikoff's attention is focused on more than just the objects to be found in the city. He is equally interested in the people who fill the streets of New York, and no encounter, however brief, is too slight to escape his notice, too banal to become a source of epiphany. These two examples, from among many possibilities:

> I was walking along Forty-Second Street as night was falling.
> On the other side of the street was Bryant Park.
> Walking behind me were two men
> and I could hear some of their conversation:
> 'What you must do,' one of them was saying to his companion,
> 'is to decide on what you want to do
> and then stick to it. Stick to it!
> And you are sure to succeed finally.'
>
> I turned to look at the speaker giving such good advice
> and was not surprised to see that he was old,
> But his companion
> to whom the advice was given so earnestly,
> was just as old;
> and just then the great clock on top of a building across the park
>
> began to shine.

*

> The tramp with torn shoes
> and clothing dirty and wrinkled –
> dirty hands and face –
> takes a comb out of his pocket
> and carefully combs his hair.

The feeling that emerges from these glimpses of city life is roughly equivalent to what one feels when looking at a photograph. Cartier-Bresson's 'decisive moment' is perhaps the crucial idea to remember in this context. The important thing is readiness: you cannot walk out into the street with the expectation of writing a poem or taking a picture, and yet you must be prepared to do so whenever the opportunity presents itself. Because the 'work' can come into being only when it has been given to you by the world, you must be constantly looking at the world, constantly doing the work that will lead to a poem, even if no poem comes of it. Reznikoff walks through the city – not, as most poets do, with 'his head in the clouds', but with his eyes open, his mind open, his energies concentrated on entering the life around him. Entering it precisely because he is apart from it. And therefore this paradox, lodged in the heart of the poem: to posit the reality of this world, and then to cross into it, even as you find yourself barred at all its gates. The poet as solitary wanderer, as man in the crowd, as faceless scribe. Poetry as an art of loneliness.

It is more than just loneliness, however. It is exile, and a way of coming to terms with exile that somehow, for better or worse, manages to leave the condition of exile intact. Reznikoff was not only an outsider by temperament, nurturing those aspects of himself that would tend to maintain his sense of isolation, he was also born into a state of *otherness*, and as a Jew, as the son of immigrant Jews in America, whatever idea of community he had was always ethnic rather than national (his dream as a poet was to go across the country on foot, stopping at synagogues along the way to give readings of his work in exchange for food and lodging). If his poems about the city – his American poems, so to speak – dwell on the surfaces of things, on the skin of everyday life, it is in his poems about Jewish identity that he allows himself a certain measure of lyrical freedom, allows himself to become a singer of songs.

> Let other people come as streams
> that overflow a valley
> and leave dead bodies, uprooted trees and fields of sand:

> we Jews are as the dew,
> on every blade of grass,
> trodden under foot today
> and here tomorrow morning.

And yet, in spite of this deep solidarity with the Jewish past, Reznikoff never deludes himself into thinking that he can overcome the essential solitude of his condition simply by affirming his Jewishness. For not only has he been exiled, he has been exiled twice – as a Jew, and from Judaism as well.

> How difficult for me is Hebrew:
> even the Hebrew for *mother*, for *bread*, for *sun*
> is foreign. How far I have been exiled, Zion.
>
> *
>
> The Hebrew of your poets, Zion,
> is like oil upon a burn,
> cool as oil;
> after work,
> the smell in the street at night
> of the hedge in flower.
> Like Solomon,
> I have married and married the speech of strangers;
> none are like you, Shulamite.

It is a precarious position, to say the least. Neither fully assimilated nor fully unassimilated, Reznikoff occupies the unstable middle ground between two worlds and is never able to claim either one as his own. Nevertheless, and no doubt precisely because of this ambiguity, it is an extremely fertile ground – leading some to consider him primarily as a Jewish poet (whatever that term might mean) and others to look on him as a quintessentially American poet (whatever *that* term might mean). And yet it is safe to say, I think, that in the end both statements are true – or else that neither one is true, which probably amounts to the same thing. Reznikoff's poems are what Reznikoff is: the poems of an American Jew, or, if you will, of a hyphenated American, a Jewish-American, with the two terms standing not so much on equal footing as combining to form a third and wholly different term: the condition of being in two places at the same time, or, quite simply, the condition of being nowhere.

We have only to go on the evidence. In the two volumes of *Complete Poems* (1918–75), recently published by Black Sparrow Press, there are a surprising number of poems on Jewish themes. Poems not only about Jewish immigrant life in New York, but also long narratives on various episodes from ancient and modern Jewish history. A list of some of these titles will give a fair idea of some of Reznikoff's concerns: 'King David', 'Jeremiah in the Stocks: An Arrangement of the Prophecies', 'The Synagogue Defeated: Anno 1096', 'Palestine under the Romans', 'The Fifth Book of the Maccabees', 'Jews in Babylonia'. In all, these poems cover more than 100 pages of the approximately 350 pages in the two volumes – or nearly a third of his total output. Given the nature of the poems he is best known for – the spare city lyrics, transcriptions of immediate sensual data – it is strange that he should have devoted so much of his writing life to works whose inspiration comes from *books*. Reznikoff, the least pretentious of all poets, never shows any inclination towards the scholarly acrobatics of some of his contemporaries – Pound, for example, or Olson – and yet, curiously, much of his writing is a direct response to, almost a translation of, his reading. By a further twist, these poems that treat of apparently remote subjects are among his most personal works.

To be schematic for a moment, a simplified explanation would be as follows: America is Reznikoff's present, Judaism is his past. The act of immersing himself in Jewish history is finally no different for him than the act of stepping out into the streets of New York. In both cases, it is an attempt to come to terms with what he is. The past, however, cannot be directly perceived: it can only be experienced through books. When Reznikoff writes about King David, therefore, or Moses, or any other Biblical figure, he is in effect writing about himself. Even in his most light-hearted moments, this preoccupation with his ancestors is always with him.

God and Messenger

The pavement barren
as the mountain
on which God spoke to Moses –
suddenly in the street
shining against my legs
the bumper of a motor car.

The point is that Reznikoff the Jew and Reznikoff the American cannot be separated from one another. Each aspect of his work must be read in relation to the *oeuvre* as a whole, for in the end each point of view inhabits all the others.

The tree in the twilit street –
the pods hang from its bare symmetrical branches
motionless –
but if, like God, a century were to us
the twinkling of an eye,
we should see the frenzy of growth.

Which is to say: the eye is not adequate. Not even the seen can be truly seen. The human perspective, which continually thrusts us into a place where 'only the narrow present is alive', is an exile from eternity, an exclusion from the fullness of human possibility. That Reznikoff, who insists so strenuously in all his work on this human perspective, should at the same time be aware of its limits, gives his work a reflexive quality, an element of self-doubt that permeates even the most straightforward lyric. For all his apparent simplicity, Reznikoff is by no means a primitive. A reductionist, perhaps, but a highly sophisticated one – who, as an adroit craftsman, always manages to make us forget that each poem is the product (as he put it in one work) of 'hunger, silence, and sweat'.

There is, however, a bridge between time and eternity in Reznikoff's work, a link between God and man, in the precise place where man is forced to abstain most vigorously from the demands of the self: in the idea of the Law. The Law in the Jewish sense of the word and, by extension, in the English sense. *Testimony* is a work in which reading has become the equivalent of seeing: 'Note: All that follows is based on the law reports of the several states.' What Reznikoff has observed, has brought to life, is the word, the language of men. So that the act of witness has become synonymous with the act of creation – and the shouldering of its burden. 'Now suppose in a court of law', Reznikoff told Dembo in their interview, 'you are testifying in a negligence case. You cannot get up on the stand say, "The man was negligent." That's a conclusion of fact. What you'd be compelled to say is how the man acted. Did he stop before he crossed the street? Did he look? The judges of whether he is negligent or not are the jury in that case and the judges of what you say as a poet are the readers. That is, there is an analogy between testimony in the courts and the testimony of a poet.'

Trained as a lawyer (though he never practised) and for many years a researcher for a legal encyclopedia, Reznikoff used the workings of the law not only as a description of the poetic process, but also, more basically, as an aesthetic ideal. In his long autobiographical poem, *Early History of a Writer*, he explains how the study of the law helped to discipline him as a poet:

> I saw that I could use the expensive machinery
> that had cost me four years of hard work at law
> and which I had thought useless for my writing:
> prying sentences open to look at the exact meaning;
> weighing words to choose only those that had meat for
>   my purpose
> and throwing the rest away as empty shells.

> I, too, could scrutinize every word and phrase
> as if in a document or the opinion of a judge
> and listen, as well, for tones and overtones,
> leaving only the pithy, the necessary, the clear and plain.

Testimony: The United States (1885–1915) Recitative is perhaps Reznikoff's most important achievement as a poet. A quietly astonishing work, so deceptive in its making that it would be easy to misread it as a document rather than as a piece of art, it is at once a kaleidoscopic vision of American life and the ultimate test of Reznikoff's poetic principles. Composed of small, self-contained fragments, each the distillation of an actual court case, the overall effect is nevertheless extremely coherent. Reznikoff has no lesson to teach, no axe to grind, no ideology to defend: he merely wants to present the facts. For example:

> At the time of their marriage
> Andrew was worth about fifty thousand dollars;
> Polly had nothing.
> 'He has gone up to the mine,
> and I wish to God he would fall down
> and break his neck.
> I just hate him.
> I just shiver when he touches me.'
>
> 'Andy, I am going to write a letter that may seem hardhearted:
> you know that I do not love you
> as I should
> and I know that I never can.
> Don't you think it best
> to give me a divorce?
> If you do,
> I will not have to sell the house in Denver
> that you gave me,
> and I will give you back the ranch in Delta.

After we are divorced,
if you care for me and I care for you,
we will marry again. Polly.'

*

Jessie was eleven years old, though some said fourteen,
and had the care of a child
just beginning to walk –
and suddenly
pulled off the child's diaper
and sat the child in some hot ashes
where she had been cooking ash cakes;
the child screamed
and she smacked it on the jaw.

It would be difficult for a poet to make himself more invisible than Reznikoff does in this book. To find a comparable approach to the real, one would have to go back to the great prose writers of the turn of the century. As in Chekov or in early Joyce, the desire is to allow events to speak for themselves, to choose the exact detail that will say everything and thereby allow as much as possible to remain unsaid. This kind of restraint paradoxically requires an openness of spirit that is available to very few: an ability to accept the given, to remain a witness of human behavior and not succumb to the temptation of becoming a judge.

The success of *Testimony* becomes all the more striking when placed beside *Holocaust*, a far less satisfying work that is based on many of the same techniques. Using as his sources the US Government publication, *Trials of the Criminals before the Nuremberg Tribunal*, and the records of the Eichmann trial in Jerusalem, Reznikoff attempts to deal with Germany's annihilation of the Jews in the same dispassionate, documentary style with which he had explored the human dramas buried in American court records. The problem, I think, is one of magnitude. Reznikoff is a master of the everyday; he understands the seriousness of small events and has an uncanny sympathy with the lives of ordinary people. In a work such as *Testimony* he is able to present us with the facts in a way that simultaneously makes us understand them; the two gestures are inseparable. In the case of *Holocaust*, however, we all know the facts in advance. The Holocaust, which is precisely the unknowable, the unthinkable, requires a treatment *beyond the facts* in order for us to be able to understand it – assuming that such a thing is even possible. Similar in approach to a 1960s play by Peter Weiss, *The Investigation*, Reznikoff's poem rigorously refuses to pass judgment on any of the atrocities it describes. But this is nevertheless a false objectivity, for the poem is not saying to the reader, 'decide for yourself', it is saying that the decision has already been made and that the only way we can deal with these things is to remove them from their inherently emotional setting. The problem is that we cannot remove them. This setting is a necessary starting point.

Holocaust is instructive, however, in that it shows us the limits of Reznikoff's work. I do not mean shortcomings – but limits, those things that set off and describe a space, that create a world. Reznikoff is essentially a poet of *naming*. One does not have the sense of a poetry immersed in language but rather of something that takes place *before* language and comes to fruition at the precise moment language has been discovered – and it yields a style that is pristine, fastidious, almost stiff in its effort to say exactly what it means to say. If any one word can be used to describe Reznikoff's work, it would be humility – towards language and also towards himself.

> I am afraid
> because of the foolishness
> I have spoken.
> I must diet
> on silence;
> strengthen myself
> with quiet.

It could not have been an easy life for Reznikoff. Throughout the many years he devoted to writing poetry (his first poems were published in 1918, when he was twenty-four, and he went on publishing until his death in early 1976), he suffered from a neglect so total it was almost scandalous. Forced to bring out most of his books in private editions (many of them printed by himself), he also had to fight the constant pressures of making a living.

> After I had worked all day at what I earn my living
> I was tired. Now my own work has lost another day,
> I thought, but began slowly,
> and slowly my strength came back to me.
> Surely, the tide comes in twice a day.

It was not until he was in his late sixties that Reznikoff began to receive some measure of recognition. New Directions published a book of his selected poems, *By The Waters of Manhattan*, which was followed a few years later by the first volume of *Testimony*. But in spite of the success of these two books – and a growing audience for his work – New Directions saw fit to drop Reznikoff from its list of authors. More years passed. Then, in 1974, Black Sparrow Press brought out *By The Well of Living & Seeing: New & Selected Poems 1918–1973*. More importantly, it committed itself to the long overdue project of putting all of Reznikoff's work back into print. Under the intelligent and sensitive editing of Seamus Cooney, the sequence so far includes the two volumes of *Complete Poems*, *Holocaust*, *The Manner Music* (a posthumous novel), the first two volumes of *Testimony*, and will go on to include more volumes of *Testimony* and a book of *Collected Plays*.

If Reznikoff lived his life in obscurity, there was never the slightest trace of resentment in his work. He was too proud for that, too busy with the work itself to be overly concerned with its fate in the world. Even if people are slow to listen to someone who speaks quietly, he knew that eventually he would be heard.

Te Deum

Not because of victories
I sing,
having none,
but for the common sunshine,
the breeze,
the largess of the spring.

Not for victory
but for the day's work done
as well as I was able;
not for a seat upon the dais
but at the common table.

                                                    1974; 1979